LIFE, HABITAT AND PEACE

LIFE, HABITAT AND PEACE

Prof. Fani Bhusan Das

PARTRIDGE

To order additional copies of this book, contact
Partridge India
000 800 10062 62
orders.india@partridgepublishing.com

www.partridgepublishing.com/india

TABLE OF CONTENTS

Dedication ix

Acknowledgement..xi

About The Book xiii

Introduction xv

LIFE

- Life Is A Song Of Love 1
- Recognize Life 5
- Redesigning Of Humans...7
- Life And Matter 10
- Union Of Life..13
- Life & Energy 15
- Creation Of Life...17
- Life & Untold Stories 19
- Life And Mahatma 21
- Life & Relationships...23
- Life & Social Capital 25
- Life And Education 27
- Truths Of Life 29
- Life And Development 31
- Life And Einstein..33
- Life-Matter And Spirit 36
- Life And Spiriton..38
- Human Existence- Basics Of Life 40
- Life And Spirituality...42
- Life And Time..44
- God And Life 46

- Life And Consciousness.................................49
- Life And Conflicts 51
- Neural Wiring And Life...............................55
- Reform Education, Reform Life....................58
- Dissolution Of Life 61
- Simplicity Of Life......................................63
- Complexity Of Life....................................65
- Life And Mind...67
- Life and Death..69

HABITAT

- Habitat Space To Live 73
- Culture Of Habitat 75
- Deterioration Of Habitat...........................77
- Habitat-Our Life 79
- China-A Clean Habitat? 81
- Smart Habitat-Six Indicators.......................83
- Pleasant Habitat 87
- Development-Pledges Of Paris (Cop-21)...................89
- Make Existing Habitat Smart 91
- Polution And Small Steps 97
- Past Wrong Doings 99
- Positive Indicators For Habitats..................101
- Climate And Habitat 104
- Global Impact On Habitat..........................107
- Climate Hazards And Habitat.....................109

PEACE

- Peace And Civilization 117
- Bhutan And Peace 124
- Learning the lessons to live on Earth in Peace 126
- Peace & Management 130

- Political Parties And Governments – Peace, Violence And Prosperity. 134
- Peace Education 140
- Prelude To Nature's Fury And Human Violence 142
- Justice & Peace 146
- Biosphere Peace Movement (BPM) 150
- Relevance Of Idea Of "Success Of Peace" In Today's Technologically Complex Wired World. 156
- Peace Calendar – 13 Moon 28 Days A Perfect Harmony Of Time 158
- Happiness And Peace For Social Order 164
- Peace And Hunger 169
- Peace & Violence 187
- Peace Energy And Antimatter 192
- Conflicts & Terrorism 200
- Family & Peace 205
- Spirit Of Peace 207
- Sustainability Of Peace 215
- Energy & Peace 224
- Inner Peace 229
- Peace And Human Rights 232
- Peace Poems 238

About The Author 249
Epilogue 253

DEDICATION

Dear Lord, the book and ideas are all YOURS. Everything in the Universe belongs to YOU. How can I dare to offer anything to You LORD? However still I offer this book at your feet. Pardon me for this and bless the ideas of the book to ignite the minds of world citizens to initiate positive changes keeping in view humanitarian and ecological values.

Acknowledgement

I am indebted to Dr. T. P. Ray, an internationally reputed Psychiatrist who inspired me with his ideas on mind and spirit. His experience in different Habitats of the world and mental and social status of those people has also given me valuable inputs. Architect K.B.Mohapatra, Piloo Mody College of Architecture, Cuttack, Odisha, India provided me support and library facilities for the book to whom I express my high regards and gratitude. I also express my appreciation to Mr.Saswat Raman Sahu, Founder of AllGraphik and Mr. Sudeepta Saha & Mr.Saswata Debadutta who designed the sketches for insertion in the book. I am also thankful to Mr.Manoj Mohapatra who has supported me fully with computer work of my manuscript. I am grateful to Partridge, A Penguin Company who took all care to publish my book.

About The Book

How can I write a book when I do not know "who am I"? However, according to HIS direction, the book enlightens the life of Human species and the world and how they live their life in stinking Habitat devoid of peace. Both "inner" life & Peace and "outer" life & Peace; their living Spatial environment-the Habitat are all HIS design and direction. Readers of the book will find UNIFICATION of HIS gift of Life, Habitat and Peace.

I hope the book will serve as academic purpose as well as make a beginning of changing the human psychic towards redesigning of Habitats where life is safe, secured, sustainable and peaceful with unification of Life, Habitat and Peace. The basics of such a change are possible only through blending of "Science of Matter" with "Science of Spirituality". Time has come now for our life to accept Spirituality as Science to ensure that Matter should not overtake mind and Spirit. Virtual and vulgar prosperity for few at the cost of millions of poor people can no longer be tolerated. There is no doubt that if prosperity for few continues, the world will be fractured and life will be distorted. This calls for unification of life, habitat and peace. The book has attempted to convey key ideas of Life, Habitat and Peace in nutshell to ignite and mutate the human minds for evolution of ideas towards a sustainable, prosperous and peaceful world and humanity.

INTRODUCTION

This book contains the gospels of Heavenly Father to which everything in this universe belongs. ONENESS of Life, Habitat and Peace is complete with blending of "Science of Matter" with "Science of Spirituality. As the world is becoming more and more complex day by day, HE, the Supreme Energy has reappeared (appeared before also when the world was about to be dissolved) to infuse ideas in human minds to save the world from dissolution for continuance of existing civilization. The ideas in the book provide impulses to understand life- its joys, sorrows and activities in the present materialistic positive world and how to overcome the turmoil of life by developing a sense of enoughness and empathy discarding anger, ego, jealousy, self-glorification, pride, intolerance, self interest and all negativities of the world. The sense and purpose of Habitat is lost today. The entire global space has become violent, vulgar and virtual, economically, socially, physically and environmentally. It has lost its connectivity with Mother Nature; as a result Nature is becoming nasty and taking revenge on human species in an unimaginable scale. The ideas of the book suggest some measures to reconnect man with Nature through reforming the Habitats. War, terror, violence, killing and all kinds of vices today are destroying the harmony of human species and depleting vigorously the integrity of ecology and its resources on which the humans depend for their survival in the Habitats. The word "PEACE" is now out of the dictionary of humans, as a result God's ONENESS of Life, Habitat and Peace is broken in to pieces. Violence in every sphere of life is full leaving no space for peace. It is really to wonder how human mind accepts that they can live without peace- the ultimate reality of life. The book has also deliberated on many issues of peace especially how to genetically improve the electro-chemical secretion of Serotonin etc in the mind to remove the word "violence" from human dictionary. Finally, I leave it to Heavenly Lord to deal with such life threatening crisis, the world is facing today. HE only knows what is going to happen. The ideas of the book belong to HIM. I being a miniature fraction of the universe, made an attempt to generate ideas for the future analyzing the present crisis.

LIFE

01
Life

LIFE IS A SONG OF LOVE

Life is a song of love. Everyone should sing it. Life is also ocean of sorrow. Everyone should cross it. Life is serious, it is not a joke. Every moment of life should be taken seriously by taking proactive steps to eliminate disease and disorder of life. If it is neglected mountains of sickness both mental and physical and disorderliness will overtake. By that time one is helpless. The best way to spend life is to sing song of love internally and spread love externally. For doing this some of the suggestions are-

1) Connect the inner and the outer-tap into your essence and act from a place of personal alignment to affect real outer change.
2) Become an "energy master"-the key to peace building and recognize energy processing style.
3) Identify and deal with all forms of bulling.
4) Stand in fire of opposing views and feel whole as well as hold space for others to do same.
5) Transform fear and anger in yourself and among others into mutual trust and compassion.

6) Cultivate listening and dialogue to co-create a culture of peace in your family, work place, organization and community.
7) Identify and heal old wounds in yourself and for loved ones, colleagues and community members.
8) Develop a strong foundation in community building and organizing skills.
9) Manifest your greatest qualities in service to humanity's emergence.
10) Connect with an inspiring network of peace builders, friends and allies around the world.
11) Play a significant role to global peace initiatives and celebrations.
12) Reestablish connectivity of life with Mother Nature.

Those are some of the basic formulas to sing song of life. Try, you will find the solace.

In the path of life's journey, time comes when you are depressed and frustrated. Under such circumstances one has to surrender before you, Dear God, because there is no alternative. Relations and friends depart you and you are left alone. This is the time one likes to go to YOU as everything is out of control. Life's body, mind and soul remain fractured because of relation/friend ego remain adamant and rock like hard. OH! Heavenly Father why do you create such a situation when one is deprived of joy and divine presence. Everything of life -body, heart and soul are yours. But still I am helpless. Dear Lord Help me to overcome such painful time in the life. YOU have blessed me so much in my life; I do not know how to express my gratitude. Everything in this world/universe belongs to you. What more I can offer you? I only beg for the well being of future generations. Help them with wisdom with the help of which they will be able to lead a happy, peaceful and prosperous life contributing to others welfare and well being. How can one live in isolation and alone? Dear God just HELP such people and tell them to obey the laws of Mother Nature.

Love also embraces Consciousness which is a function of brain. It is not in the brain. The Forebrain is responsible for functioning of the Consciousness. Sub consciousness is like information stored in the computer which can be easily retrieved. Unconsciousness is the sum total of information stored in the satellite which is difficult to retrieve, but can be retrieved. If you can access unconsciousness, with which you are extremely powerful to access any information and knowledge.

Life is also a fragment of "spirit" (energy) and "matter" which provide basic raw materials from Nature for the humans to live on earth. Spirit is the is the creative energy which infuses life in inert matter and key to a healthy and peaceful life. But, unfortunately the "greed" for "matter" has upset the relationship between life and Nature. Due to inappropriate application of "Spirit" (Spirituality) with "matter", life today is becoming more and more virtual. Technological advancement has brought many benefits to human life but it has also created many adverse impacts on life. The most critical impact is drifting away from humanitarianism and laws of Mother Nature resulting in serious types of Natural and health hazards. Time has now come for sustainable and peaceful unification of life, Nature, technology, habitat, peace and above all the Heavenly Father and Mother so that life sings songs of love for all time to come.

Life is a song,
love is the music.

Life is a Song of Love

02
Life

RECOGNIZE LIFE

Can you answer the question "Who are you"? You, I and all in the world are fraction of our Dear Lord without which we are zero. HE has gifted us two elements of design- The Heart & The mind which work in harmony with each other in a living body. We have to take advantage of this and make our thought and action creatively constructive. This is the reason your hands gently move to Heart & Brain to express your gratitude to the SUPREME ENERGY. If you learn the blending of science with spirit, your knowledge expands and you find answers to many problems/joy/pleasure of your life's journey. Today life has become extremely complex. Intra-family and Inter-family relationships have been strained. The "inner" pollution has become more than "outer pollution". Understanding level has come down. Anger, ego, jealousy, selfishness, pride, self-glorification, craze for money and matter etc have overtaken all qualities of humanitarianism transforming human species in to a different kind of species.

With such drastic change, would you like to discover the secret to the simplicity of "connecting your heart and mind"? When you look around the world, it is difficult to recognize life, which has become distorted by developing two faces; one "inner" and other "outer" which in most of the cases are opposite to each other. True life is that where "inner' face equals to "outer" face and duality is removed.

Heart and mind are two most crucial gifts of God to life, which should be unified to change the present nature of humans. Heart pumps and supplies blood to all organs of the of the body to keep life functioning. But, unfortunately the current violent environment has transformed the present life into a curse for which it is difficult to recognize humans, which is the unique gift of God in the Biosphere. The present recognition of life has to change, failing which all of us will be condemned for posterity. Let our heart and mind collectively ignite IQ (intelligent quotient), EQ (emotional quotient) and SQ (spiritual quotient) to restore back to original life created by God.

Life has become so complicated, even we and our own relations do not recognize each other. During the transition from childhood to youth and then to old age, equation of life changes drastically to recognize only self and not anyone else. It is time for true recognition of life which is a mini fraction of God with Nature as its Mother. Spread this message across the world to change the behavior of humans.

REDESIGNING OF HUMANS

Redesigning of Humans is continuously taking place in the pathway of hominid evolution starting from homohabilis to homoerectus to the present state of homosapiens. Evolution of hominid from pongid occurred as it is seen that hominid skull bears marks of a way of life strongly different from pongids. There is upward displacement of the braincase relative to face due to increased flexion of the basicranial axis. These changes facilitated to maintain balance of head consequent to development of erectus postures and bipedal gait. Such modifications result in the expansion of the braincase accompanied by increase in the ratio of brain weight to body weight. There is expansion of cerebral cortex to become highly complex organ for receipt, integration and discrimination of sensory information and for coordination of motor activity. In addition to brain volume, organization of brain tissue is also very crucial. Then came the stage of conceiving ideas in the minds of hominids creating tool of both functional and aesthetic values. From the study of fossil examples, it is observed that average capacity braincase has increased from 640CC(Homohabilis) to 1450CC(Homosapiens). The mean cranial capacity of Homosapiens has also increased to about 1350 cubic centimeters from less than 1000cc in case of Homoerectus. All these variations are primarily due to pressure of adaption to environment to lead a distinct ways of life. This study is indicative of power of brain to create environmental niches and also to adapt changes.

Today in addition to environmental factors, the man-made technological factors are also playing a crucial role. The use of computer, mobile and other electronic goods is also going to change human body shape and size, along with the mind. It is predicted that use of computer by hand does not require a long hand, the humans have now. May be in thousands and million years time, the length of human hands may be smaller. Similarly the functioning of mind may also change. Although studies are taken up through computer to find out the causes of such changes, there is no specific interference to resolve the truths. But one thing is sure that the present human life style and functioning are going to redesign the human body structure and shape, besides mind. As scientists say mind is the main instrument that runs the body organs. Consciousness which is outside the mind determines the behavior, attitude and differentiates between right and wrong. Mind is said to be creative cosmic energy and life which is conditioned by mind is the result of consciousness of mind. Consciousness cannot be computerized but use of computer may change the pathway of hominid evolution. It is therefore necessary to be aware of the impact of both man-made and environmental influence to direct the redesign of humans in the right direction. Today with the impact of major environmental changes like climate change, global warming, deforestation, sea level rising and increasing greenhouse gases etc and man-made technological development like computer etc, it will be difficult to predict how the changes will redesign the humans in future. But evaluating the present trend, there is every likelihood that in few years time, the humans will be redesigned by the greatest of the great Architects-the Creator.

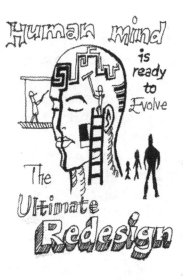

Redesign of Humans

04
Life

LIFE AND MATTER

Strictly materialist science is contributing to mental health problems among youth. Many depressed teens that hurt themselves don't possess the "hallmarks of a psychiatric disorder," wrote Baruss, quoting a Toronto Star article titled "Psychiatrists see rise in suicidal teenagers." "Instead they seem to be suffering an existential crisis that is sort of 'I'm empty, I don't know who I am, I don't know where I'm going, I don't have any grounding and I don't know how to manage my negative feelings.'" Barušs wrote: "Scientific materialism assures us that reality is a meaningless, incidental, mechanistic, collocation of improbable events." He summarized some of the ways in which the materialist interpretation of reality has already broken down: quantum events are seen to be non-deterministic; time is no longer linear, as effects have been shown to precede their causes; particles change position depending on where one looks or what one decides to measure. Although, we have improved materially to acquire money and comfort, we have declined comparatively more to have happiness and peace. Matter derived from Mother Nature is pure to satisfy basic needs of life. But technology when blended with Nature against the laws of Nature creates a matter which is destructive and distorts the original life. Distorted matter from Nature lacks consciousness and makes minds polluted. See, what is happening to our children and people in general. The products of polluted technology void of conscience, affect us, our children and other people who are dedicated and intimately involved with mobile, TV Laptop etc as a result their eyesight is affected. Their Spinal cord which is part of the brain is also truncated affecting both mental and physical health. In mobile they listen songs, see videos of many varieties even porno besides getting connected with girls at early age. It is really painful to observe, how our next and present generation destroying their own quality of life. I think we all are responsible for such situation. The society, parents and seniors are all silent and not providing them with right advice. Parents are busy in earning money (For Whom God only knows), seniors are scared and the society is dumb. Policy makers/ politicians are busy to collect votes and make money to continue their chairs at any cost even at the cost of their own children. Technologists make inventions blindfolded without caring for the serious consequences; their technologies would impact the human capital. They are only interested in name, fame and money. It appears in such disastrous situation, what can be done to save the humanity? Then who will do it? But we are proud of our so called development where people sitting idle at home get free food and they do not want to work. This makes their mind idle and we know that "idle mind is devils workshop". With idleness, they succumb to all illegal and unethical activity like violence, drugs, murder, rape and robbery etc besides in many cases being addicted to drugs, alcohols etc youths and people in general run over people and killing them while driving either in two wheeler or four wheeler. Only answer is to develop "work ethics and culture" without unhealthy competition so that they become positively productive without remaining idles. They must work and get their two square meals. Will any one listen to this?

05
Life

UNION OF LIFE

Way back in 1978, when I joined LBS Academy of Administration at Mussorie for my training, the first lecture was on YOGA. A young man between 25-30, who was called "Sadhaka", came from the base of Himalaya talked to us about YOGA. His first sentence was "YOGA IS BLENDING OF BODY, MIND & SPIRIT TO AROUSE YOUR CONSCIOUSNESS TO MINIMIZE YOUR DOMINANT "I" FOR EMBRACING "YOU" & "US" WHICH IS PROCESSED THROUGH HEART & MIND". AND THIS WILL KEEP YOU IN GOOD MENTAL & PHYSICAL HEALTH., DO NOT FALL INTO THE TRAP OF commercialization of yoga.

This is what today is happening to Yoga. That is why you are not able to come out from "I" and go to "YOU" & "US" for which you are ignorant of real self. This is the main reason of today's disturbed world-- conflicts are increasing and happiness is declining. The true Yoga teachers must convey this message to the students and then teach different positions of Yoga. Then only humans will change and dominant "I" will leave space for YOU & US. Physical fitness is only one of the dimensions of Yoga, but remember emotional and spiritual dimensions are more crucial to bring about changes in human thought, behavior and actions. With this you will holistically heal, purify and unify yourself with the Universal energy to bring happiness and peace in your own life as well as others life. Only then you contribute to welfare of the planet earth and the humanity as a whole. Yoga establishes connectivity and relationship between all as Yoga is peace, not power. Peace cannot be attained through power, yet power is the result of peace.

Realize that life is very short and understand true Yoga to leave your foot prints for improving your own and others quality of life through your physical, mental and spiritual fitness understanding that Yoga is amazing conduits of energy and positivity. Yoga provides ideal "collective of minds" for nourishment that binds life, habitat and peace creating harmony between lives and laws of Nature.

Yoga is purely scientific. But today many people are trying to make it a business, which is really painful, as Yoga tries to bring harmony within the mind and spirit of the body and make one feel establishing union with the Creator. Yoga should be made mandatory in the schools so that the children grow up to become worthy citizens of the world for enrichment of future.

Life & Energy

Energy is life without which we cannot exist.

One can live in two energy sphere- Positive & Negative. We should live from our Positive Energy of Heart & Mind. Today it appears more people live from Negative Heart & Mind Energy. Because of this, the present Environment is highly polluted and Violent. Eating, Education and Environment are critical to convert negative energy in to positive one. What we eat, what education we are given and in what kind of Environment we live-- all the 3Es will determine the kind and level of Energy basing on which our Heart & Mind operate.. Positive operation will result in peaceful and sustainable living where as Negative operation will result in Violent, Vulgar and Virtual (3Vs) living. Basing on this a strategy can be formulated to replace the negative energy of heart and mind in to positive one for a quality living with love, affection, empathy & Truth, Order and Harmony-- a holistic peaceful and sustainable living at both individual and to global level.

Energy is that which makes a thing move. Energy creates peace as well as hydrogen/nuclear bomb. Every biotic and abiotic components use energy for consumption and transformation to other forms, structure and shape. Energy is essential for all kinds of life to live in the world. But it is unfortunate that humans have not understood the basics of energy which is generally positive in nature. They find more pleasure to use energy in negative ways to create destructions. In the course of evolution, human mind is becoming more and more negative. Such attitude not only kills self but also bring devastation to other lives. Peace is drifted away, leaving the humans to live a miserable and violent life. Unless humans turn away from negative energy to positive one, time is not far away when they will be wiped out from the habitats.

There is an hierachy of energy. Absolute Consciousness Energy-The Creator which trickles down to cosmic energy, spiritual energy, consciousness energy, conscious energy and matter energy. They all play significant role in life as well as in habitat and depending on the kind and level of energy, peace or violence dominate in the world. It is always desirable to activate positive energy through which quality of life improves to design suitable habitat embraced with peace.

CREATION OF LIFE

Creation of life is mystery, we know only fringe of it. How sperms compete to break the seal and dashed against the ovum to fertilize it to create a life is a mystery. Who created the sperms and ovum and from where life entered the fertilized ovum? Many questions are to be answered. "God Particle" scientifically discovered was also a part of interaction, but who and what is God- the most vital question remained unanswered. Is God is the Supreme Source of Energy from where everything emerges? In any case, it has not been answered since the beginning of creation and it will not be answered in future to come. We have to end up in "Belief System" & "Faith". We may accept one perception that "God is the Supreme form of Energy" beyond which no energy exists. HE is the Supreme Creator and Architect.

We have to understand that when there is creation, there will be dissolution. We are not going to live forever. Keeping this truth in mind, we have to navigate our life. Do not be after "excesses" in life which will bring you more pains and frustrations. You will lose the basis of creation and become violent in every stage of your life. Develop a sense of "Enoughness" for everything in life and then only you will justify your creation.

It is a wonder wherefrom energy entered the life. What kind of energy has been applied to form parts of life and to operate the parts. Is it the gift of Supreme energy –The God? When we are busy in our day to day work, we have no time or desire to know wherefrom we have come. I think God through Mother Nature had designed a process for the creation of life, which is really complex. However when there is creation, our activities in the Habitat should ensure wellness of Life for which Habitat design should be socially, economically, physically and environmentally pollution free. In turn, the quality of life improves to allow Peace to prevail.

We are advocating many theories for creation of life. Invention of God particle is one of those theories. But in this concept there are many question and ultimate question is "Who is God and where from HE came ruling the universe for billions and billions of years"? I do not think this question will be answered scientifically at any point of time till the existence of life. Philosophically, one can only try to proof the status of the Creator, but still it may not convince all. But in any case, we have believed in supernatural power as we are not able to answer the questions relating to creation of life and the world as a whole. Creations should be honored by the created lives and goods to establish value-based human society.

Life & Untold Stories

I find people do not have courage to tell you just "NO". They will not misbehave with you but tell you stories to say ultimately NO. Human behavior is changing fast. Their genes of Heart and neurons of Mind are restructured; may be because of negative environmental factors. I was with some senior citizens. They were talking of their youth days. One gentleman said during those days we were very bold. If we are to say No to anything even a girl, we straight say no. But today they do not say NO, but make stories to trap a girl and manipulate to say YES. This is a dangerous change in human behavior. No one believes no one and a circle of "belittling others" begins. Truth takes a back seat. Ego dominates and some sort of competition to prove that "I am the greatest" begins. In every sphere of life negativity dominates which is becoming worst day by day. We forget that life has come with empty hands and returns back (where?) also with empty hands.

My driver was driving the car and taking a left turn. From the back a motor cycle dashed my car. A teen who was driving the motor cycle came rushing to the driver of my car and demanded compensation for the damage of his motor cycle. Then police intervened and told the teen to come to his senses and told him rather he should pay compensation to my car driver as per laws. The teen argued for some time and he came to his senses after talking to his parents. It only made me thinking how teens are provided with what kind of education; and kinds of experiences they are exposed to. Such small things to be taken care of for building the education system to develop humanitarianism in today's human society. Two things bother me in the life system of today-increasing violence and deteriorating relationship between man and woman. Violence ranges from domestic violence to global violence. Absence of mind set of compromise; adjustment and tolerance are some of the key issues need to be addressed. It starts from individual "Inner self" to community, societal and global sphere. Our leaders are misguiding the humanity for their self interest. They fail to study human mind and heart which actually mold each and every activity carried out in the world. PLEASE REMEMBER LIFE IS A GAME OF HIDE AND SEEK IN THE LIMITED SPACE AND INFINITE TIME. Both TIME & SPACE should be utilized with application of POSITIVE ENERGY to make the world livable and peaceful for its inhabitants.

LIFE AND MAHATMA

Many decades ago the world was ignited with a new light which has illuminated the world till today and will be illuminating future generations on a continuous basis..Yes, Mahatma Gandhi- the highest value of HUMAN CAPITAL assessed today and for all time to come. He is a simple, ordinary, spiritual soul devoid of ANGER, EGO, JEALOUSY, VIOLENCE, VULGARITY, VIRTUALITY, MATERIALISTIC & GREED culture, dedicated his life for others.

He is an ignited Energy for the well being and welfare of all human beings and sons and daughters of Mother Nature. Discrimination between man and woman was not in his dictionary. He loved from his heart "MOTHER NATURE" for which he said "INDIA LIVES IN VILLAGES". Time runs. Today in what kind of TIME we are? It appears we have diverted from the path Mahatma was leading. Young India and young generation of today have to go back to Great Mahatma and live their lives according to his vision.

He is the Role Model for the World will remain as Role Model for generations to come.

Life and Mahatma

10
Life

LIFE & RELATIONSHIPS

All of us have to enhance the value of human capital. Strengthen the family bondage, respect and obey parents and other members of family- SHED ANGER, EGO, JEALOUSY, DEVELOP A SENSE OF ENOUGH NESS, ESTABLISH PEACEFUL RELATIONSHIP between your inner self and with parents, brothers, sisters, wife, your children and all other relationships to bring about high rate of growth to your capital(human). Develop empathy, feel for others, respect others emotion, make your heart fill with love and affection, love Mother Nature and all her products. Do not allow to enter the impulse that "I AM THE GREATEST" in your mind. Be humble, EGO LESS, ANGER LESS like Mahatma and always extend your heart and soul to eliminate others sufferings. Do not show off and give rise to CONFLICTS. Do not make false publicity to deform the life of people. Relationship has to be designed to HEAL, PURIFY AND UNIFY one's inner-self and others mind, body and spirit. Do not cultivate or promote vulgar and unethical relationship between man and woman. OH! Young India, young Indians and world citizens adopt the above vision -you will be able to build a strong Social Capital to live in harmony with each other in the world. If you can do it, then only there is some sense of economic capital; otherwise it is useless and fooling around. Relationship also depends on behavior which is determined by the words you express and your body language. For delivery of a task, one can use both rude and sweet words. Communication skills should be developed so that relationship is managed with sweet words. With rude words you not only hurt others but delivery of task will not be as per your instructions and time. It has also adverse impact on your health because of your irritation and dissatisfaction. Quality of life depends on quality of relationship. Words, ways of expressing words and body language etc decide relationship. If all these are positive, one develops wonderful relationship, as a result life is more happy and peaceful.

Life

A bundle of eternal spirit

Enable people to live life

Not in isolation

But with number of companions

A collective mind is created

To deliver

Civilization goals

Being managed through cordial relationship

Free of ego, anger, jealousy & load of wellness ship.

11
Life

LIFE & SOCIAL CAPITAL

Social Capital & Human Capital- Are we interested? Or only swayed by so called materialistic capital giving rise to 3Vs--- Violence, Vulgarity and Virtual. The so called economic growth is meaningless if we do not build Social & Human Capital. Let us adopt ultimate objective of development as strong and sustainable building of Social & Human Capital and not as % economic growth. There are many ways to achieve this; but there should be people to listen this message and change their approach to development & growth. How many such people will come forward?

Are we progressing forwardly or backwardly? The later is true. Making high talks or delivering provocative lecture to thousands of people is no progress. We announce high promises, but forget to implement those promises when come to power. It is really very sorry state of affair. We are yet to understand that education & health are two basic sectors on which development of other sectors depend. We are fooled by promises of proposals of investment in billion/millions and waste our votes. There should be amendment of Constitution providing that if a political party does not fulfill the promises after coming to power, that party should be blacklisted to contest next election.

Like USA, the Prime Minister/Chief Minister's tenure should be for two terms only. Then only new blood will come with new governance and ideas. I think this is the key to prosperity and peace for all citizens.

The basic objective of Economic Plan is to improve Human Capital as well as Social Capital which in turn will deliver higher growth rate to the economy. Therefore it is necessary to decide priority of allocation of funds with wisdom. If we we only harp upon higher rate of economic growth, the youths and people will be violent, drug addicted, adopt gun culture and involved in all kinds of anti-social activities, then what is the sense of high economic growth? Similarly in the society if there is more violence, disharmony, conflicts, absense of community feelings, higher economic growth looses its glory. It is a fact that relationship with good behavior, body language and sweet communication skill will make life happy and satisfying. It also helps to go up in the ladder of your career simultaneously upgrade the quality of both Human Capital and Social capital. The resultant impact will be a healthy, happy and peaceful life and society/country for improving quality of life of people.

12
Life

LIFE AND EDUCATION

Education in India has taken a back seat for which the country is in turmoil. Teachers are not behaved properly. They do not enjoy a status like doctor, engineer or I.A.S in the society. In developed countries Teachers are highly respected and enjoy high status in the countries as a result human capital and social capital are strongly built. But still they are confronted with many problems like societal and humanitarian etc.

Our previous generations including primitive ones were much happier than what we are today. They were honest, sincere, truthful, harmonious, caring & sharing with positive values embedded with strong emotion and spirituality through education. They were taught to love Mother Nature and never tried to harm her. They were breathing pure air, drinking pure water and living in unpolluted land. There was no gender discrimination and a great Harmony existed between man and woman. They were happy and peaceful. Today everything has reversed because of out dated education. We are progressing backwardly. Let us realize this and change our approach to development and growth. Let us be positive and not hypocrites and do what we speak. Blend IQ, EQ and SQ to go back to our olden days so that happiness and peace are restored. This will mean real prosperity and not the virtual, vulgar and violent prosperity of today's development.

Education must start from womb and continue throughout life till one reaches the grave. It is not a one time job. With advancement of time, almost everything changes. In order to cope up with changes, one needs education. Reading books is a must for upgrading one's life. But today computer has taken up this role, to which youths are more attracted. In no case the computers will effectively take away the culture of "reading books". Education needs concentration and patience and also good and dedicated teachers. The teachers should be given high status in the society so that they live a good life. Then only the students will come up to the mark. Parents have high responsibility to improve the education standard of their children. They should not leave everything to teachers/schools. We have to remember that a country can develop well through only improving the standard of education through parents and quality educational institutions. The Habitat must also facilitate spatially for smooth and accident-free mobility. Education should be fully supported by Life, Habitat & Peace to create high quality of Education system.

13
Life

TRUTHS OF LIFE

I want to ask the World Human Community-What they want- Prosperity inequitably distributed like sitting on the top of the Nuclear Bomb about to blast accompanied by glittering buildings, infrastructure, automated and digital, vulgar and violent life style with ugly Social & Human Capital- Violence, Kidnapping, Killing, torture & murder, rape, Single Mom, de-fathering, children at risk, high handedness of authorities, domestic violence victimizing women and men, sexualizing the society to break the basic morals to be Humans and many other negative attributes. OR A tranquil Social & Human Capital living in harmony and peace with each other and Mother Nature without any violence and immoral attributes, prosperity with a sense of enoughness without any discrimination and with adequate attention to development of mind, body, spirit, emotions, building the bridges of relationships, Zero-conflict, due respect to Ecology-the provider of resources for growth, friendly government genuine interest to solve problems and not simply war of words and last but not the least empowering both Social & Human capital for healing, purifying and unifying all the positives to blossom the human life to an entity of peace & prosperity creating a peaceful, moral, sustainable and beautiful human society drenched with humanitarian values. If your answer is the first one, then continue with the present tyrant system and if your answer is to the later one, then change the present system of government, executive, judicial, media and all other wings of governance which call for making Social & Human Capital as the foundation basing on which economic growth is to be designed and not the vice-versa.

I am a dreamer of truth

As healthy life live on truth

I am not the only one

Many people join me

To discard the derivative of untruth

For the world

To live in oneness.

14
Life

LIFE AND DEVELOPMENT

The basic meaning of Development is "Change" which is always in a continuous process with time. The human mind has to work out what kind of changes are required at a particular time. It appears human mind is now distorted as the changes they are initiating are leading more towards destruction than construction. My Mind asks me what is happening to the human species. As if Economy and abundance of money are everything to live a life. The economic development for prosperity (which is virtual) has ruined the human society as well as the Ecology on which we depend on for economic development. This mind set needs to be reversed. Base should be SOCIAL DEVELOPMENT & HUMAN DEVELOPMENT on which economic development should be planned. Do not transform the human body in to a machine and society as a foul game field. Holistically incorporate MATTER & SPIRIT in human activities. Adequately take care of mind, emotion, intellect, ego (positive), anger (negative), limitless desires (negative) and Consciousness & Conscience etc for Social & Human development and THEN, plan economy accordingly. This is a global challenge. If the big people of the world will not do this, the history will record them as dangerous enemies of humanity. This change of planning approach will remove all the problems we are facing today like poverty, pollution. Inequity, unequal access to resources, destruction of ecosystem etc besides problems like disruption of family life, deterioration man-woman relationship, Kidnapping, violence & killing, amassing ill-gotten wealth, over-sexualization of the society, cheating in the name of God, corruption, waste of TIME & SPACE by war of words, immoral thoughts and actions. The negative impacts of electronic goods like mobiles, TV, etc and purely materialistic approach to life etc must be discarded. Do not be proud of things invented which kill the humans mentally and physically. Do not market and spend huge money for advertising objects and ideas detrimental to healthy growth of humans. THINK ABOUT THIS & CHANGE OUTLOOK TO PUT PRESSURE ON BIG PEOPLE OF THE WORLD TO CHANGE THEIR APPROACH OF PLANNING STARTING FROM SOCIETY--HUMAN AND ONLY THEN TO ECONOMY' AND NOT VICE-VERSA.

Life is a growing tree, It needs inputs for growth

Development is the input, to support growth of life

Develoment be in conformity, with laws of nature

To make life and development sustainable & peaceful

15
Life

LIFE AND EINSTEIN

I have not named the great Scientist who desired to blend Consciousness/ Spirituality with Matter. You must have identified him-he is Albert Einstein. People do not accept/adopt any change immediately. TIME & SPACE are two factors which determine when the Change/ idea will be adopted. Continuing with consciousness, I would like draw attention to the providential statement of the great Scientist who wanted to invent an equation linking Consciousness, Compassion with Science. He realized it late in his life and could not do it as there was no TIME & SPACE for him in this bitter earth. His soul departed with lot of dissatisfaction as he was not very happy with the equation E= mc square. I have tried to derive an equation in which infinity moving energy characterized by healing, purifying and unifying Matter, Life as well as Spirit will be able to ignite the mind for Creative Construction (not destruction) only to remove Virtuality, Vulgarity and Violence to build Social Capital & Human Capital for sustainability and to create a peaceful world. The equation is "Absolute Energy of Consciousness = s (compressed matter & antimatter) - a molecule of positronium to the power of m(all kinds of matter) x e(all kinds of energy) Which is multiplied by t(time-healing, unifying and purifying) to the power of infinity. This equation links development of material world with Spirituality through hierarchy, exchange and up and down movement of energy flow in Energy Pyramid for sustainable and peaceful development to create a harmonious world where all people of the world live in harmony and peace without any kinds of conflicts. This implies at Zero ground level that all kinds of material development must have a dimension of Spirituality in the design, implementation and management processes. This can be achieved by igniting the mind to see with inner vision and to realize that five sensory elements of humans belong to the common treasury of spiritual imagery (beyond the physical and emotional planes). Now I express my ideas on Spirit/ Spirituality. Spirituality is to be perceived not as abstract or religious related issue but it is based on purely scientific basis. To begin with it has direct linkage with TIME, SPACE, ENERGY & MATTER, all these four dimensions deteriorate without Spirituality. That is what is taking place today across the world. To understand Spirit scientifically, like atom, the fundamental particle of Spirituality is "SPIRITON", the nucleus of which is "CONSCIOUSNESS ENERGY PARTICLE" around which UNIVERSAL THOUGHT & EMOTION particles revolve. These particles are responsible for operation of ATOM & CELL (fundamental particle of LIFE). and if you see with Inner Vision, all these are directly or indirectly controlled and regulated by Absolute Energy of Consciousness which we respect and worship as GOD. Consciousness is energy particle which determines the quality of life. Considering this Einstein message to humankind is "Live a simple life".

Einstein's idea of gravity waves has now been recognized. When the Einstein's dream of waves of Consciousness energy will be recognized? That was his last dream before his death. The gravity waves can penetrate anything in their path unlike light, ultraviolet, X-rays, radio waves which are absorbed by dust and gas which make much of the universe hidden. Equation of Consciousness wave energy has been discovered, but yet to be recognized. Once it is recognized, the world and life will change making everything in tune with the Harmony of the Universe. It calls for accepting "Spirituality" as Science. Waves of Consciousness Energy and Spirituality will drastically change the human minds developing spirit of "oneness" with the Universe, thus contributing, penetrating and permeating the life of individual for striking the fine chord of harmony playing in the universe.

16
Life

LIFE-MATTER AND SPIRIT

Unification of Matter and Spirit (energy) is the key message to humans for application in their day to day life for improving the quality of values in their lives. First, I deal with Matter. In the material world, there are three ordinates namely Security, Comfort with a sense of Enoughness and Happiness are the priorities. Security comprise of safety of life, of food, of shelter and of all other socioeconomic and environmental needs for the humans. The second ordinate is comfort which implies a state of ease for physical well-being. There is no limit to comfort, for which I emphasize it should be with a sense of enoughness so it becomes inclusive covering all human beings. The third, Happiness is a state of mind and the output of quantity and quality of Security & Comfort provided through spirit and matter. As you know, the fundamental particle of Matter is Atom which creates all kinds of material objects. This is scientifically proved and there is no confusion about this. Therefore the three ordinates are basic material needs for humans to live. Atom can be both creative and destructive. We have to ensure that Atom/Matter is utilized only for Constructive purpose. But it is not happening in real world. More and more it is used for destructive purpose. This necessitates Spirit to be blended with Matter to wipe out or eliminate use of Matter from killing people through various approaches like terrorism etc, destroying the ecosystem and creating imbalance between Natural, Domesticated and Fabricated environment.

The life is run by mind and spirit. If any one of them becomes dysfunctional, life stops. We cannot see spirit but we can see the matter. Matter has a great role to influence spirit determining the quality of life. Spirit is a unique energy that has the power to create life and matter. As the matter is created by atom (fundamental particle of Matter), spirit is created by Spiriton (fundamental particle of Spirituality), which has consciousness as nucleus around which universal thought and emotion particles revolve. The matter provides various kinds of products to satisfy our senses have both positive and negative impacts. Today it is observed that negative impacts are increasing. First the negative impact encapsulate the mind & heart through which spirit loses its original structure and becomes radical and creates many kinds of bottlenecks to obstruct smooth running of life. It is therefore essential to take extreme caution to eliminate radical spirits by controlling universal thought and emotion and use matter in conformity with laws of Mother Nature.

17
Life

LIFE AND SPIRITON

Yes, time has to reverse back beyond 1840A.D. when fundamental particle of Matter- "Atom" and fundamental particle of Spirit- "Spiriton" were blended together to make both material and spiritual objects of the world. After 1840 A.D. spiriton was removed from the intellect of humans and only Atom has created and creating all the material objects that we see all around us till date. Energy which evolves Matter in to life is ignored in our day to day activity as a result the use of SPACE has become disorderly. This has become a threat to man's whole intellectual dominion over Nature. I think it is now TIME to embed the present state of the physical sciences in to a long term historical setting and by doing so, we can weave together in to a more coherent intellectual fabric of Spirit- Matter branding to change the ingredients of different kinds of development currently taking place in the areas of physical thoughts. This will enable us to design and use of SPACE more effectively for making the outputs more sustainable and peaceful and free the Space from Virtuality, Vulgarity and Violence for evolution of "SMART" HUMAN CIVILIZATION. Earlier, I said life recycles and the quality of life depends on level of spirit one operates. My thoughts revolve around the concept of Blending of Science of Matter with Science of Spirituality. Life is linked to Matter, basically Security, Comfort (with a sense of enoughness) and happiness and life is evolved from Spirit, the basics of which are Truth, Order and Harmony. All components of Matter are run by lowest level of man-made Energy and all components of Spirituality are organized by higher level of Energy-- the highest level is Absolute Energy of Consciousness-- THE GOD.G stands for generation, O stands for operation and D stands for dissolution. It is a cycle- anything that is generated operated within the parameters of Time & Space and dissolution takes place and again generation---and the cycle continues. We cannot see Energy, for that matter we cannot see GOD but when our failure is absolute we surrender to God and give physical shape to it as our intellect is not developed till date to see Energy. The TIME, up to the year 1840 A.D, English name for scientists was "natural philosophers" which was a holistic concept of Spirit & Matter. As a result all products of "generation" were to a great extent sustainable & peacefully operated. The TIME 1841 A.D. is the turning point of human civilization as Science and Philosophy intellectually separated in to two separate spheres. SPIRIT, LIFE, TIME & SPACE evolve differently and the intellect of humans started "creation" of a "Material World" devoid of philosophy. Evolution and Creation adopted two different paths and continuing till date accumulating problems after problems increasing the miseries of human civilization. Now TIME has come to reverse back and blend Science of Spirit with Science of Matter to secure a stable place for the humanity in the Biosphere.

18
Life

HUMAN EXISTENCE-
BASICS OF LIFE

My mind is bit disturbed. With passing of time, concepts, values and ideas are changing. I think there are some basics of life like Truth, Order & Harmony blended to security, comfort and happiness; from which various values emerge do not change. In most of the cases the so called leaders project themselves as Role Models for others to follow. But if you look "inner" depth of so called leaders, one will, without any bias find that they are hollow and lack of knowledge and wisdom. If such people are the engines of change what is going to happen to Social Capital & Human Capital? Both capitals become incapacitated to conceive the role of natural resources and principles of ecology and bring disaster to human society. Virtuality; Vulgarity and Violence in each sector of life dominate which deform the thoughts and actions of humans. There is increasing differences and consensus becomes a day dream on any issue concerning human welfare. Such deterioration of Social & Human capital seriously and adversely affect the harmonious functioning of neurons and body Cells and convert human species into an instrument of "Creative destruction". We have to identify true Role Models whose hearts and souls are for welfare of people, economy, environment, government, quality of living and mobility, which only can usher an era of "Smart Human Civilization". I do not think after so many billion years of human existence, true meaning of life has been invented. There are many concepts of life scientifically, philosophically, religiously and psychologically advocating meaning of life, but still the mystery of life continues. Life is a spirit. Where from the Spirit comes, we still wonder. Why and how the spirit takes different forms and shape. What is the relationship between life and shape? How the formation of brain and mind and thought process of each and every individual is different. Life born from same womb and parents are also different. I think it is difficult to answer all such questions. But one thing is true that is LIFE, TIME & SPACE are inter related and are products of interaction and blending of different forms of ENERGIES-Absolute Energy of Consciousness, Cosmic Energy, Spiritual Energy, Consciousness Energy, Conscious Energy and Matter Energy(the lowest form of energy invented by humans). It implies that there is a hierarchy, exchange and up and down movement of various energy flow, perhaps in a pyramid form. Energy of any kind we cannot see, but when they interact with TIME & SPACE, life germinates. Time, a celestial unit blended with space and environment gives meaning to Life and continuously in the change mode from the beginning of the universe. MEANING OF LIFE REVOLVES AROUND ENERGY, SPACE & TIME. It can be conceived as a Cosmic unit of Universe, as every life is a mini-universe and produced by production unit of infinity size with parts, components and inputs of Energy, Space & Time which are varying and evolving on a continuous basis.

LIFE AND SPIRITUALITY

I have evolved a new concept "Blending of Matter with Blending of Spirituality". We all know all about Science of Matter- all objects all around us and all kinds of products that we produce. All the products of Matter glitter so much that we have become blind to everything except Matter. It appears it is leading us to pure materialistic world where there is no life, no place for love, affection, emotion, empathy, caring-sharing, spirit and soul etc- only a materially glittering & saturated life. Do you think Life is merely "a sugar-coated glittering mass"? The answer is absolutely NO, as it is evident from the misery and suffering, the humanity is passing through. There is a missing link to be a human. The missing link is the "SPIRIT" which makes us to live, think, work, create and recreate, to run our mind and all kinds of movements with full positiveness. From "SPIRIT", the word "SPIRITUALITY" emerges. Many now interpret as abstract, religious, making no sense for the scientific world of Matter and useless. What a human perception, for which we are suffering and our thought process is directed negatively. I advocate "SPIRITUALITY IS SCIENCE"- a highest form of cosmic energy which creates everything in the world including humans and the world. You know well that without energy nothing can move and take shape. I define Spirituality as "SPIRITUALITY IS ABSOLUTE AND INFINITE SOURCE

OF CREATIVE ENERGY WHICH IGNITES HUMAN MINDS WITH POSITIVE THINKING AND EMOTION;ESTABLISHING EQUILIBRIUM BETWEEN SPIRIT, MIND & BODY FOR MORAL AND MATERIAL OUTPUTS WHICH WILL LEAD THE HUMANITY TO PROSPERITY WITH HAPPINESS & PEACE FOR ALL BIOTIC & ABIOTIC COMPONENTS OF THE BIOSPHERE.' Adopt Spirituality as Science (WHICH I HAVE PROVED IN MY BOOK OF "PEACE TIME CALENDAR, (Published in USA) and blend it in your day-to-day work and life dealing with Matter, you will find the difference and your life becomes a blessed one and ever cheerful. No negativity will come near you. Do you not like to live such a blissful life? I think everyone wants but they were not finding a way. However, now they have a clear, distinct, emotionally and spiritually charged path. Do make a trial.

Life is still a mystery

I do not know

Who created it

How it is created

But it appears to me

As an illusion of Spirituality & Matter

Yet, I wonder

If ever I can realize life

With the connectivity of

Spirit, Mind, Body and Matter.

LIFE AND TIME

LIFE & TIME- how closely they are intertwined- Life consists of PAST, PRESENT &FUTURE. When time passes it becomes PAST, when time is NOW, it is PRESENT and when we look ahead it is FUTURE. Today the world has become complex and monocentric and the Humans think there is no past and future and now is the only time we can do and undo things. Because of infatuation to Now, we have transformed human body into a machine-its mind, emotion, empathy, love, intellect, ego, soul and spirit etc are thrown out. Like a machine, I, ME & MINE dominate and perform only for self benefit and totally ignoring or forgetting the needs of others- their physical social, economic and environmental, besides spiritual needs. Hurting others through your five senses is a great sin. Be sweet talkers, humble and listen to others with all respect. Do not bring anger, greed & jealousy during all such activities. We are so mad about NOW, that we forget about past and future But. NOW need to be designed accumulating and learning experience from past, incorporating only positives of the NOW, and then only we can look to the FUTURE with Hope for a humanitarian culture..TIME from Childhood to old stage change continuously-physical, moral and spiritual process etc. If the Time of childhood, youth and old stage is blended with Science of Matter with Science of Spirituality, all the three stages of LIFE and TIME become meaningful for peace to prevail. Otherwise in every stage one suffers and the world is deteriorated. I quote a great lesson of life- "An old man told his grandson "My son, there is a battle between two wolves inside us all. One is EVIL. It is anger, jealousy, greed, resentment, inferiority, lies and ego. The other is GOOD. It is joy, peace, love, hope, humility, kindness, empathy and truth. The boy thought about it, and asked "Grandfather which wolf wins?" The old man quietly replied "The one you feed". "We are visitors to this time, this place we have just passed through. Our purpose here is to observe, to grow, to love.....and then we return home. "(Australian Aboriginal Proverb)". That exactly what we are. But we behave as if this is our perennial Home and do or undo any kind of thing; more of creative destruction and act like victors. We have to change ourselves so that during our stay here we behave like visitors and recognize the value of time. Abdul Kalam has said "Life and Time are the world's best teachers. Life teaches us to make good use of Time and Time teaches us the value of Life"

Life is like a stream of river

Flows calmly or with humping and jumping

Which changes life from time to time?

And makes me to live on earth.

21
Life

GOD AND LIFE

We are always on outside journey. What we see outside today a bundle of negativity, violence, fractured Mother nature, pollution of sky, land and ocean and 7 billion unique human species who are composed of ego, anger, jealousy, intolerance, impure, ready to strike others, disharmonious, breaking unity of their own group and hypocrisy. With all these, we are racing towards the end of journey, where there is no World. We are also searching God outside, which we will never get. Once we are able to visualize God, all the ills stated will be solved. Where is God?

Try to make a journey to your "INNER SELF"--you have to activate your thought process and meditate to go deep to your inner self-if you can, the experience of outside journey is erased and you see a sparkling clean sky with bright stars, a purified land and ocean, eye-soothing "GREEN" and above all billions of life forms living in harmony with each other in a purified and unified environment and all on a sudden you come face to face with GOD and there only GOD resides. You are excited and then calm down to transform yourself to true human being creating and recreating collectively with GOD. Don't you want this INSIDE JOURNEY? Do this, you will find GOD as a result the world becomes Heaven. Everything will become in a state of happiness and peace. Mind; basically make you understand what is good, what is bad. Spirit of empathy and the understanding "what hurts me would feel the same way to you" and many other positive and negative attributes of life are the outputs of functioning of mind. Scientifically, in the left brain an almond shaped mass of gray matter known as amygdala is associated with strong emotion like fear, empathy, love and affection etc. In the left brain also, medial prefrontal cortex is linked with emotion and social thinking. The damage of this part leads to belligerent feelings. The anterior cingulated cortex located also in the left brain increases activities of deficient moral dilemma, signaling the dorsolateral prefrontal cortex in the right brain to provide executive control. Dorsolateral prefrontal cortex is associated with cold cognition and it becomes more active when people make more utilitarian choices leading to dehumanization by exploiting morality for evil purpose. It is therefore necessary and challenge of the day to regulate your brain parts for reverting to the path of humanization.

Mind is also creative cosmic energy. Its perceptive power is created by the force working in the matter of the biosphere. In this force and the matter, the sub-conscious and unconscious minds work which not only create themselves but also life and holistic mind. The mind, spirit, body of life of a person depends on the physical principles of mother Earth. Life is conditioned by matter and is the result of three consciousness of mind. One of the basic sources of power of mind is thought, keeping his/her internal body functioning and the consciousness deciding right, wrong, moral, immoral etc. The challenge of today is to recognize devils of a person like ego, selfishness, anger, jealousy, violence, indifference to others sorrow, indifferent attitude, stressing only on "I", "ME", "MINE", injustice, immorality, inability to recognize consciousness, truth, order and harmony etc and create thought waves by igniting all three consciousness to kill the devils so that true humans and humanitarian qualities are restored. This will enable us to create a high quality human resource which in turn will create a beautiful, peaceful and sustainable world worth living in. Keep Consciousness energy always at the back of your mind and heart that will always guide you as a fraction of God particle.

God And Life

22
Life

LIFE AND CONSCIOUSNESS

Do you know we have three minds- Conscious, Sub-Conscious and Unconscious? We all think, speak and act and almost do everything from conscious mind. Mere conscious mind is arbitrary, hardly with any rationality. Sub-conscious and unconscious minds are more powerful. The quality of world and its human resource is today on decline because the humans are not able activate their sub-conscious and unconscious minds to make the conscious mind more orderly by integrating brain parts more harmoniously. In the sub-conscious and unconscious minds which are buried deep in our brain are full of positiveness, purity, truth, order and harmony. All real great people of the world could access to these two minds and express & act through conscious mind with wisdom. All the evils of the world like violence, terror, inequity, anger, jealousy, rigidity, pornography etc are increasing because of our inability to access sub-conscious and unconscious mind. The roots of all problems we are facing in the world as we are our unable to draw power to conscious mind from sub-conscious and unconscious minds. There are many ways to draw power from sub-conscious and unconscious minds. Specific Mind training exercises will be able to do it. The basics are make your thought process always positive, remove anger, jealousy and rigidity, love everybody, be empathetic even to your worst enemy, shift your focus from money and material to spirituality etc. Try this, you will live a happier and peaceful life. It is not limited to this only, but a qualitative Human Resource will positively evolve for the betterment of the world.

I wonder who I am.

I have looked at life from both sides

From up & down

Still somehow

My ignorance perturbed me

To access Consciousness

Which makes me to

Think, talk & work for whom I do not know

Still I do not know what consciousness is

I look at blue sky, Blue Ocean

In search of Consciousness

But it eludes me

I continue without knowing consciousness

And my ship of life sails

Where I do not know.

$$\frac{23}{\text{Life}}$$

LIFE AND CONFLICTS

The world is in crisis today. Conflicts are everywhere--in politics, society, economics, environment, tradition, culture, technology, education, judicial and so on. What the humans want and what is there ambition? The worlds need a qualitative human resource that can minimize/eliminate the conflicts. Man-Woman relation is now at flux generating various types of conflicts. Government intervention in every sector of human life is increasing as a result societal, family, economic and environmental values are adversely affected. Today my mind is agitated on two issues (besides many others) relating to woman and Man. There are different values in different countries. In one of the countries of the world two decisions have been taken recently-1)Single Mom- A girl may produce a child without marriage and she is not compel to declare the name of the father 2) Porno sites in electronic and other media—can it not be stopped?

On issue No1, What is freedom- a girl can have sex with number of boys but it will be difficult to know which boy's sperm has made her pregnant. She gets a baby without knowing completely the type of gene her baby is made up. After the death of her parents (if she had at all), the hurdles she will face is unimaginable. But she will definitely face trauma, as a result the quality of her life is going to be disastrous and collectively, the quality of human resource will dwindle leading to collapse of the world. This is evident from the daily media reports-almost daily girls are committing suicide due to unethical relationship between boys and girls, rapes are very common and electronic media relationship in many cases leading to break down of lives etc. There will be many other adverse impacts on the society. On issue No2, can you imagine what will happen to the mind set of teenagers? Sex is intoxicating- leave aside teenagers, it creates mental aberration in adults even. Teenagers mind and body will become like a monster and they forget everything about their studies and values except the porno and materialistic positive visuals, as a result the quality of human resource is going to decline to zero level. Then who will manage the world? A chaotic world will commit suicide out of total frustration. People invented computer and minting money and then to wash their sin they are donating Himalayan size money they have accumulated for health, education etc. Will health & education will improve-Absolutely no. New virus "Zika" (consequence of our lop sided development) has surfaced on earth to create more conflict in life People must do something that porno and highly materialistic visuals are not circulated by all media including mobile phones, computer, besides taking other measures to save poor teenagers and thereby making some efforts to improve/ restore quality of human resource to save humans and the world which are now facing more serious situation than a Nuclear Bomb. Many may not agree to my point of view, but one should seriously think about this to bring about changes in the decaying society for incorporating "morality" in our mind set.

I think a mass movement must start throughout the world to deal with these two issues. I hope there will be great deal of responses to oppose the two issues. What is friendship? Today if you agree with me and I agree with you, then we are friends. Otherwise friendship breaks and conflict arises. Friendship is a holy word and it continues till life exits. We should realize the difference between the true and virtual friends. Electronic friendships have raised serious problems throughout the world even to the extent of rape, killing, murder and other kinds of act of violence along with some positive effects also. Exchange of ideas is not friendship. However it may be intellectually good. Best way to make friendship is to make your soul's dearest friend. He will not cheat you or harm you. What is needed today is to befriend with God, besides other good souls which will be eternal friendship. From this position one may resolve conflict between person to person and only then the relationships are sustainable. Once conflicts are resolved and violence is eradicated, relationship between person to person and country to country will improve.

Life and Conflicts

24
Life

NEURAL WIRING AND LIFE

The Thought Process makes us what we are. Mind generates thought waves that mold our own lives and others lives. It appears that today neural wiring of our brain are short circuited creating instability in our thought. We are facing confusion to decide what is right and what is wrong. This needs to be corrected again by the same thought process. Which were good last 50 or 100 years back are today bad and which were bad are now good. This is simply aberration of our minds. It is time that we become more conscious about directing our thought process in a more articulate manner, so that we are able to decide right things and do the same to save the humanity from the "doomsday" that will wipe out the species Humans from the biosphere.

As you know, MIND is very complex-till date no one in the world has clear perception about mind. Still then I try to ignite my mind to find out the reasons for the activities of humans which are only for "Creative destruction". Many new technologies instead of serving as a boon for humans are destroying the roots of human culture. There is competition by all the countries of the world who will be No.1, in the process of creative destruction. Common citizens of the world understand this but they are helpless as there is no one to listen to their agony. Unless the humanitarian values are restored by some kind of holistic profession, (give a suitable name to it) the output of all other professions will continue to be creatively destructive. All of us seeing and experiencing it but remaining silent and indifferent. We have to wait for radical change of our mind set and rewiring of our neurons. Silence is the best medicine today. With silence, you are able to concentrate only in your "inside" and disconnect yourself with the dirty world outside-- characterized by total loss of humanitarian values, breaking down of families and relationships etc. I think the world has almost lost everything even to call ourselves as "humans". When you look inside, you try to be at peace ignoring today's status of the world. Billions of neurons of your Mind process the impulses through interconnecting and interacting with number of neurons (not yet known to us) and then provide response. Genes inherited from previous generations play a very critical role interacting with the environment. The equation GENOTYPE+ ENVIRONMENT= PHENOTYPE in general dictate your IQ, EQ & SQ. If the GENE is very strong, the environment cannot counter it, you become Bin Laden. I have seen this with many people even a mother kills her relationship with her children- just imagine the power of gene. I have also seen people have totally changed their genes with the influence of environment- normally bad genes are reformed with the force of environment. Both the above category is dependent on the quality of education imparted. The later ones through input of education become quality human being and collectively create a qualitative human resource and change the world to make it worth living. The former ones with cumulative accumulation of bad genes become so rigid that they cannot comprehend right things and sticking to negativity throughout their life. Such people form a negative human resource and not only destroy their own life but destroy the whole world. In this case, the Education has to find some way of reform which still now has taken a back seat. Appropriate reform incorporating peace in education has to be taken up which is a challenge for the humanity. Can it be done? We have to start research and take action to improve the quality of both gene and environment so that future is protected.

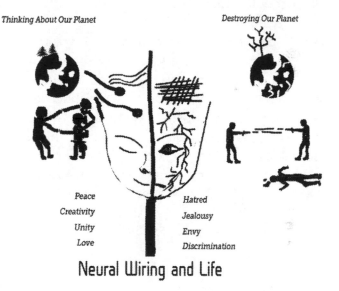

Thinking About Our Planet

Destroying Our Planet

Peace
Creativity
Unity
Love

Hatred
Jealousy
Envy
Discrimination

Neural Wiring and Life

REFORM EDUCATION, REFORM LIFE

Spirit, Mind and Consciousness are three of the main attributes that rule and blend education with spirituality. Mind is ignited by Spirit and in turn Mind produces different forms of consciousness from waking consciousness and the ultimate potential form of consciousness entirely different.....No account of the Universe in its totality can be final which leaves these other forms of consciousness quite disregarded. From waking consciousness (part of spirituality) to higher level of consciousness are all molded by education. The type education we impart must establish strong relationship between Spirit, Mind and Consciousness. Then only the education is holistic to strengthen the process of spiritual healing caused by erosion of values of life

Not spiritual education but spirituality when blended with education delivers a desirable world of humanity. We have to find ways to strengthen education system through integration of "Spirituality" and "Matter" and by incorporating it in all the professions of the world. Some of the spiritual attributes like-a positive mental attitude, a sound physical and spiritual health, harmony in human relationship, freedom from anger and fear, hope of achievement, faith development in a positive manner, empathy, willingness to share and care, labor of love, open mind to all views, self discipline, capacity to understand people and their views, spiritual finance to develop "Matter" etc are needed today. While keeping the blending process in mind, many other things are to be in the vision like- Spirituality as an instrument of healing, truth, order, honesty, justice, purity, joy, happiness, peace etc through which "Matter" goods will be produced to create a highly qualitative human resource. This should be the foundation for reforming education system.

Power of Spirit & Mind need to be conceived by leaders of Education as the foundation of development of mankind. Education without spiritual component lead to emptiness of life, devoid of fulfillment, enjoyment and laughter, of a life without love and the other emotions that make life worth living. From the play school level, students should be exposed to love, affection, empathy, feeling for others, love towards trees, shrubs, creepers, flowers etc for showering a sense of belonging for Mother Nature which are components of spirituality. While doing so, people minds are activated. Activation of mind gives signal to neurons in the mind which on receiving the impulses, process it to "love Nature & and its Creator and creation" by establishing connectivity between millions of neurons. In any subject of "Matter" like Physics, Chemistry, Nuclear Science, Social studies, Economics, Philosophy, Psychology, Mathematics and different branches of Engineering and Medical Science etc when science of spirituality is incorporated, the students develop positive thinking attitude towards life.

Mathematics is not life, but when Mathematics is linked to spirituality, the education becomes holistic providing a life style that romance, love, laugh, develop relationship essential for living, enjoy and many such ingredients of spirituality and cure diseases accrued from "matter". Spirituality with "Matter" component teaches you to give your love unconditionally, without expectation or demands. Love spirituality for the joy of living. Only such spiritually linked education will bring about a desired change of the humanity and the world.

This should be the beginning of Education reform and continue from womb to tomb and accordingly all branches of the education need to be redrafted and reformed to create a desirable world fully educated in real sense. Are we prepared to take up this challenge? We must, as there is no other alternative to save the sinking boat of humanity.

CREATIVITY + DISCIPLINE + INTELLIGENCE = BRIGHT FUTURE AND GROWING RESPECT TOWARDS NATURE

Reform Education, Reform Life

Life

DISSOLUTION OF LIFE

Issues of same sex marriage approved by USA Supreme Court for their whole country is a beginning of a new chapter in the history of human civilization. In course of time, other countries of the world may follow it, as America has done it. The entire social environment will undergo a radical change-enrichment of society or degeneration of the society. Only TIME will say. If human is a product of Nature, is "same sex marriage" takes place in Nature? Can it be related to dissolution of the world as predicted by high-rated scientists? Sixth time dissolution that is going to take place can be the output of cumulative human actions and behaviors. I think any action against the LAWS OF NATURE will contribute to dissolution of earth. Do you think all men are bad? Recently I saw a report that a girl of about 25 years killed her husband by thrashing his head with stone, because he returned home drunk? But he did not misbehave with his wife. Later she repented and now in jail. Yes, we say females are weaker gender, but they also become very strong and rigid and sometime behave worst than men. Let us not always blame men. In 66 million years back dinosaur along with many other species were wiped out and the world was collapsed and that was the 5th time in the history of evolution such a horrible thing happened. After lot of research and study now three reputed Universities of the world- Harvard, California and Princeton predicted that collapse of the world will take place for the sixth time wiping out many species- Top of which is the HUMANS. It is only because of human action all sectors of biotic and abiotic elements of the world are being gradually destroyed. This has resulted in a Violent World, where peace has eluded the mankind. As a result, shortly we may face the consequence. The British scientist Sir Isaac Newton predicted in 1704 that world will end in 2060.

Life dissolves with time

A process of Nature

But people cry & shed tears

And console each other

Death, dissolution of life

Laughs & wonder at people

Who still hold the spirit

Within themselves

And then enjoy life as usual

And make dissolution a day of celebration.

27
Life

SIMPLICITY OF LIFE

Life is complex. Simplify it and lead a peaceful life. Some of the keys to simplify are 1)Adopt Truth, Order and Harmony for a life worth living.2)Ignite your body with organic energy generated from pure Nature and not packaged food.3)Always be under the shelter of Supreme Energy-The God.4) Empower yourself with knowledge linked to wisdom.5) Face the reality and do not fall prey to the attractions of virtual, vulgar and violent ideas and objects.6) Discard Anger and be humble.7) Do not run after greed and satisfy your needs. 8) Do not be proud of anything 9) Do not speak ill of any one which will rebound back to you, rather try to convert enemy in to friend.10) Develop family culture with ethics and relationship that is bonded with love, affection, value-based determinants.11) Take special care of kids, children and adolescent age group members in the family so that they grow up to keep up the honor of the family 12) Respect elders. 13) Be always sweet talker than vomiting bitter words 14) Establish loveable and sustainable relationship with relations and friends.15) Develop skills of "Family Management" 16) Develop the habit of Compromise, Adjustment and Tolerance. 17) Destrain on stress.18) Respect and love "Mother Nature". They are some of the keys to simplify life and to lead a peaceful life. Remember

Life is a gift of God. Do utilize it to the best satisfaction of God. You will be blessed and will live a heartfelt and peaceful life. Owner of Life is God. HE perfectly does the owner's duties and responsibility.

I have lived a life ... Making it simple

With a sense of Enoughness

Simple life makes me free of all odds

Simplicity is small is beautiful, It glorifies my life

No one walks with me in the path of simplicity

As life is dominated by

Complexity to acquire more wealth & Matter

Forgetting that one day

It will desert you and take away happiness & Peace

The little bit you had, Then you hanker after simplicity

Which drifted away from me far & far?

And I cry.

28
Life

COMPLEXITY OF LIFE

Day to day Life is becoming more complex. Relationships are changing. Life which starts from family has now become more or less disorderly. For some petty matter there are conflicts in the family. Respect to elders is declining. Children are more becoming peer oriented. Political divisive game has divided the family members. Different members of family belong to different political group giving rise to serious difference of opinion and conflicts. Further, materialistic positivism is affecting adversely harmony in family life. Marriage as a culturally accepted institution has many alternatives now like live-in relationship, gay marriage, cohabitation, one-night stand and many other forms. Such so called marriages are more attractive today but in many cases they have created catastrophe breaking the life in to pieces. Life is becoming outer faced than inner faced. Original value of life is gradually becoming more virtual. Although outer of life appear to be shining, the inner is more and more crucified leading to utter misery which is being whitewashed by outer show business. Spirituality, which was the hallmark of life now dwindling. Life is massacred day by day as a result Human capital is reducing. It is time that every citizen of the world should think and stop the deterioration of life, which is the gift of Heavenly Father to humans. Ego and conflict of interests may be the roots; earlier were suppressed. We are more democratic than earlier as a country or society, but democracy in the family is yet to evolve (there were no democracy for the women earlier). The shift may not be a paradigm, but all are drifting to individuality. Wait for the wheel of time to roll to reach all ethical goals and who knows which is golden one? God has to be the best friend right through your life. Realize the complexity of life and try to move away from it to lead a simple and peaceful life.

Complexity of life

But what for?

I am a tourist in this earth

I have come, I will go

As a tourist I see the marvels of life

Enjoy to my full heart

Sometime complexity obstruct me

I am suffocated, ready to run away, To a simple space

Where my heart & Mind dance

To my full gratification.

29
Life

LIFE AND MIND

The world that is before us today is the image of the people of 7 billion minds of the world. There is more violence than peace that has severely affected all of us in the world. Mind is life and life is mind. Have you spoken to your mind? Mind is scientific. We have still to explore it. Mind is unfathomed. Look to the unfathomed blue sky near preferably a still ocean, your mind will be filled up with unspoken languages which make a beginning of learning to your mind. All on a sudden you will find you are a different personality- a part of cosmic mind.

Personality emerges from inside strength either positive or negative. Personality when not cultivated by healthy, humble, harmonious body, Mind, Spirit, Consciousness and soul; not only you do wrong thing, but your thoughts go astray. Think about it. Life is short and all about thoughts generated by mind. The thought which is created in the brain changes with electro-chemical secretion in the brain. This takes place with change of environment and impulses received in mind which goes on changing and directing behavior, attitude and path of life. Mind is a function of brain, which produces learning process, thoughts, creativity, and ideas etc. There is debate about subconscious and unconscious mind; where as Conscious Mind is well established. Subconscious and unconscious mind exist for which we are able to retrieve back in dreams or otherwise which we have not seen or experienced in conscious mind.

Sound Mind makes a sound life, which is possible with healthy functioning of brain parts. Left hemisphere of the brain does mainly three functions-1) Behavior determined by knowledge and reasons 2) Communicates using words 3) Logical and systematic approach. Right hemisphere of the brain also has three functions-1) Intuitive & imaginative spatial activities 2) Communicates using images 3) Children need many years upbringing, care, concern, affection. Mammalian brain generates behavior modified by experience. Feelings and emotion are output of Mammalian mind. Reptile brain behavior is controlled by raw instincts which breed violence and many evils of life. Two hemispheres and mammalian brain have to be properly nourished for making the mind positive to make life happy and fulfilling. These two minds should be activated and ignited to create a recipe of genius and creativeness. Mindfulness is a highly effective technique for focusing the mind- and for keeping focused. The resulting state of "Mindfulness" can improve memory and help us to operate more effectively across a range of situations for maintaining quality of life.

LIFE AND DEATH

Death is a part of life & vice versa. There are communities in the world who celebrate Death. Death came to the door step of my brother-in law (my sister's husband) and welcomed him to HIS Kingdom. We all cried. To control my emotion, I am now trying to philosophizing the philosophy of Death. Beginning of life means marching step-by step towards THE END, which is the only truth and inevitable. My brother-in law raised his both hands and said last words of his 80 years journey "OH LORD" and dropped his hands and closed his eyes. Within few hours his mortal body was devoured by energy-THE FIRE ENERGY. He became now part of Absolute Energy of Consciousness (GOD). I visualize, he must be enjoying his nearness to God and celebrating to his full heart content. We do not know in what shape and form and where his energy will be rekindled again. My conviction is that it will. It is a matter of time.

CAN DEATH NOT BE CELEBRATED AS BIRTH? Yes in many parts of the world death is celebrated. In a village near the town of Anup in the district of Uttar Pradesh of India, when somebody dies after the age of 65 enjoying the companion of grand children, the entire people of the village celebrate death as they believe that the soul of such persons will go to heaven.

Sri Aurobinda described Death as—

"Death is a beginning of greater life

Death is spirit's opportunity

Death is but changing our robes to wait

In the wedding garments at the eternal gate"

A DEAD MAN

DOESNOT WANT ANYTHING

FLOWERS OR TEARS AND CROWD

IF AT ALL SOME OF CAN GIVE,

COME AND SEE THE PERSON TODAY

WHEN HE/SHE IS LIVING

GIVE LOVE, AFFECION TO THE LIVING PERSON

AND ALL THAT NEEDED FOR HAPPY AND PEACE.

01
Habitat

HABITAT SPACE TO LIVE

Habitat is a product of Space and Time manufactured by Human life and other forms of life and their activities. Habitat is not static. It continuously changes mainly with human activities. Humans always in search of more comfort and luxury of life mold the Habitats to serve their vested interests. New ideas, technologies from human brain emerge either for "creative construction" or "creative destruction" which determine the form and structure of the Habitats. Landmass of the Biosphere which provide space for Habitat is limited, which cannot be increased or expanded. As such, there is a holding capacity of population in the Habitats, beyond which all kinds of economic, social, physical and environmental problems erupt. This is what is happening today. While expanding the Habitats, We are ignoring the laws of Mother Nature as a result producing pollution of all kinds. There is no pure air to inhale, no potable water to drink and land is utilized in most unplanned manner and dumped with foul garbage which become an overburden on land. The nature of Habitat in turn adversely affects the human quality. Especially, the electron-chemical secretion of Human mind disrupts the thought process which derives ideas and technologies, which are violent, vulgar and virtual. Harmony between Human and Habitat is lost and ultimately the humans suffer severely initiating the destructive process of Habitats. Time has come to restore the Harmony between Human and Habitat by changing our mind set to redesign the Habitats to overcome the serious challenges of today. Redesign the Habitat to create an environment that builds better and peaceful Human Capital and Social Capital through an economy which is in conformity with the laws of environmental resources.

I am born in a Habitat

What a Habitat?

I cannot inhale pure air

I can not drink pure water

Moving around polluted land

What a space to live Life becomes suffocating

Now I am in search of a New Habitat

Where I can live

In the lap of Mother Nature

And sleep deeply in peace.

02
Habitat

CULTURE OF HABITAT

Social landscape of Habitat of human species is dominated by conflicts characterized by alienation and identify crisis with aggressiveness of religious and cultural traits. Uneven distribution of economic and military power result in multicultural groups increasing pressure on the social structures to yield more and more to heterogeneity of human race. Dominance of one group on other now become almost instinctive phenomena increasing social tension and turmoil giving rise to chain of reactive responses degenerating the value of oneness of humans. Social and Habitat changes towards unification of humanity can be carefully designed by political forces of development activating mammalian and cortex(positive) brain and subduing the reptile one which will facilitate a new strategic landscape initiating a dynamic order of equity, justice, non-violence, wisdom, truth, order and harmony within the framework of natural cycles of the biosphere.

Culture of Habitat defined social culture and social production. When there was no external intervention, social production of Habitats was produced and managed by community with spiritual forces. Today, it is theoretically supported by collective self managed processes incorporating training, participatory responsibility, organization, and active solidarity among the inhabitants, contributes to strengthen community practices, direct democratic exercise, participant's self-esteem and more vigor social existence. But at the zero ground level, any contradictions penetrate and with minimal critical sense we accept the formulations which express duality: formal & informal city, normal and subnormal housing, global enclave and marginal neighborhood. Is this the right way to manage city? The universal and inalienable human right to a place and to housing? Can we explain the mutation of human rights in to merchandise? Social rights of the Habitat are subordinated to commercial rights. Rights of few satisfied at the cost of rights of majority. Such process is counterproductive and bring only negative to human co-existence. Destruction of social fiber is taking place on continuous basis as a consequence violence, insecurity, lack of governance, social polarization and subsequent suppression of public spaces which reject genuine initiatives for increasing Habitat production. Culture of Habitat deteriorates.

03
Habitat

DETERIORATION
OF HABITAT

What is happening to our Habitats? In developed countries with all improved infrastructure, amenities, facilities and comforts of life, safety and security of life are becoming more endangered. Anybody can kill anybody anywhere. President Obama cried in public for such danger to human life. In developing countries, poverty, unemployment and lack of adequate amenities and facilities of life have plagued the life of people. Globally human activities are not conducive for growth of livable Habitats. Urban societies are becoming more violent as is evident from daily murder, kidnapping, rapes, accidents and suicides. Climate change and global warming have extremely unhealthy impact on the citizens of the Habitats. Now the Hydrogen bomb has come. Nobody knows what will be its impacts on Habitat and its people. Unplanned sprawl of urban growth is increasing land, air, and Noise and water pollution creating serious health hazards. Mere words will not solve the urban problems, but a determined political commitment is needed to improve the conditions of urban areas. It appears that global summit resolutions hardly have any impact to stop deterioration of urban complexes. High rise blocks touching peak of sky, multi layer roads network, cars increasing (may exceed human population) are mainly the nature of Habitats today. Are we really happy with all such technological marvels? Ask yourself and come up with an answer from your "inner self." Love and relationships are lost to the technological wonders. You do not know who your neighbor is. Closeness of humans is now a thing of past. Every physical structure on land of Habitat is out of proportion and scale of humanitarian society. Economy and money dominate at the cost of human values, safety and security. We can do anything to earn limitless money even at the cost of family breakdown and deterioration of husband-wife-children relationship. For whom is money is earned is a great question. Is it that Habitats are built to earn money only? Habitats are now going through a process of destruction which in long term is going to crucify life and there will be sunset for Peace. We have to change our perception of design of Habitat to make it humanitarian and an integral part of Mother Nature.

Habitat

Deteriorates

To make life hell

No one is bothered

Everyone goes their own way

In search of concrete jungle

To confront

More deadly species

Than Humans.

04
Habitat

HABITAT-OUR LIFE

"Smart" is a buzzword today. Started with Smart City, there is now Smart fashion, Smart Car, Smart TV, Smart Mobile, Smart industry and the word is used for almost everything. The word has blown into the present time and will blow out in time when it fails to deliver the outputs of smartness. In the name of smart many people/authority are trying to do something. If we look to the history, in the past many such words emerged and vanished with zero-delivery. Let it not happen to Smart. Make habitats simple embedded with humanitarian values. Do not allow high technology to overtake human values to make the habitats unsafe, insecure, unsustainable, and violent. All cities should be smart as six indicators of smart city are basic essentials for maintaining quality of life. So why select few cities for smart development and leave other cities to rot? Quality of life in all Habitats/ Cities should ensure livability with safety and security, orderliness, violent-free, pollution free with ample opportunity to work and live happily. Provision of free food or anything free will make the people's mind devil declining the quality of Human Capital & Social Capital. Using the scarce economic capital, we are now there and tomorrow we will not be there and so in no case we should leave behind such radical and irrational ideas and actions which will destroy the future generations. Instead of competition, there should be Co-creation of ideas and changes those will enable and empower the citizens to build not only smart cities but holistically a Smart Culture which will be sustainable and a way of life of the people- not prompted or managed by the government only. All human habitats/cities should be perceived accordingly and built incorporating the six indicators. We have to ensure that the concept of "Smart" is made sustainable and not allow to deteriorate our life.

Life continues

As Habitat continues

Habitat deteriorates

Life also deteriorates with Habitat

Everyone is helpless

Life becomes devoid of Peace

Unbearable

Move away in search of

Lively Life, Habitat & Peace.

05
Habitat

CHINA-A CLEAN HABITAT?

China our competitor- The report says that "Forget money, Chinese just wants cleaner office air. It is not only about salaries, promotions and career prospects- many companies in China have found that they need to offer cleaner air within their offices to lure and retain staff". A much delayed realization. What is the use of money oozing out of so called powerful development, when clean air, clean water and clean land are out of reach? Chinese have realized the basics of life air, water and land after climbing the peak of development (as said).. Is such development has any sense when the citizens cry for the basics of life? We in India should not run or compete for such development which will snatch away the basics of life on which our living depends. Think in cool mind, what kind of development we should pursue. How the growth rate of 8%,9% or 10% matter if we do not get pure air to inhale, pure water to drink and sanitized pure land to continue our living healthily and peacefully? It is time to introspect seriously the word "DEVELOPMENT" and develop new and innovative ideas so that we are not deprived of basics of our living. Simply drawing Vision plans for 2050 or 2060 are just aberration of our mind and intellect either to fool ourselves or the future generations. Restore our connectivity with the laws of Nature and its resources through which our ideas of development must channelize. Let us not repeat China in India. We are highlighting development of China. What kind of development in China where the capital city Beijing woke up to a very hazy morning on the Christmas Day with reading of the PM 2.5-the smallest and deadliest form of airborne particulate matter-crossing 500, the maximum level on the US Embassy monitor. According to whom such environment is extremely dangerous to health. Beijing is going on issuing red alert one after another. People will become sick and die for the sake of Development. Is this the kind of development we want in India? And we proudly announce that our growth rate is higher than China (not visible on the ground) which means we want to weaken our human capital and Social Capital and sacrifice people for development. This is nothing but backward progress. Let us refine our thought process and not go by statistics and numbers in virtual show up. Let the resources of the country match our expectation with a sense of enoughness and within the framework of laws of Nature to make our development sustainable, safe & secured and violent & pollution free so that like China we do not make people sick and kill them untimely.

06
Habitat

SMART HABITAT-
SIX INDICATORS

Smart City has not emerged today. In 1960," smart cities" movement was initiated in Los Angeles with roots in technology. The application of whole range of electronics and digital technologies to communities and cities, use of ICT to transform life and working environments within the region, ICTs in government systems and territorialisation of practices that brings ICTs and people together to enhance the innovation and knowledge that they offer; form the basic technological base. Besides, technological, economic and environmental changes have generated interest in smart cities including climate change, global warming etc, economic restructuring, the move to online retail and entertainment, ageing population and pressures of public finances. All such factors to a great extent depend on the capacity of individual nation but environmental changes are truly global in nature. In simple terms, anything that happens in Land, Air & Water in any part of the world affects globe as a whole. This calls for intimate global cooperation between all the Nations of the world. For example carbon emission in developed countries is quite high compared to developing countries. But, unfortunately the developed countries are reluctant to share ideas and technology to reduce carbon emission in developing countries. In other words, climate justice is denied to the Nations in need. This will not deter the developing countries to go ahead with their Development programmes which may increase carbon emission affecting both developed and developing countries in the field of climate change and global warming etc.

Cities and towns constituting fabricated environment of the Biosphere occupy only 2% of land mass of the Biosphere, but responsible for 75% of pollution endangering human lives. Here comes the role of Smart Cities. Building new Smart cities and transforming existing cities into Smart ones need different approaches to protect human civilization. It is not that simple, limiting to slogans, publicity and poster war. It is something highly technical and managerial which may need lot of Research & Development activities. It also needs the courage, conviction and determination of the governments, besides mutual support and cooperation between governments and citizens.

Six indicators of Smart City are-

1) SMART LIVING-
   (a) Culturally vibrant accompanied by Happiness & Peace
   (b) Safe & Secured for all including Women
   (c) Healthy

2) SMART MOBILITY-
   (a) Integrated ICT
   (b) Prioritized clean and non-motorized options- pedestrian & cycle path and other non-pollutant modes of transport linked to MTS like mono & metro rails
   (c) mixed modal access.

3) SMART PEOPLE-(a) 21st Century education from womb to tomb.
   (a) Inclusive society- slum less cities.
   (b) Embrace creativity
   (c) Empower people with IQ, EQ & SQ.

4) SMART ECONOMY-
   (a) Entrepreneur ship & Innovation
   (b) Productivity- Balanced Agriculture & Industry - accept and Innovate agriculture as urban activity to develop & maintain "greenness" of the cities besides food value.
   (c) Local & Global interconnection (in conformity to local culture).

5) SMART ENVIRONMENT—Connectivity with Mother Nature must be established by adopting a "Green" culture like-
   (a) Green Energy
   (b) Green Buildings
   (c) Green Infrastructure
   (d) Green Urban Planning.
   (e) Zero-pollution.

6) SMART GOVERNMENT-

    (a) Enabling supply and demand side policy.
    (b) Transparency and open data
    (c) ICT and e-governance

BASICS OF SMART CITY ARE-

(A) NOT OPEN ENDED GROWTH- LIMIT OF CITY BE PREFIXED IN TERMS OF BOUNDARY AND POPULATION. ADDITIONAL SMART CITIES TO BE BUILT IF MORE PEOPLE DESIRE TO STAY IN URBAN AREAS.

(B) USE OF DIGITAL TECHNOLOGY LIKE INFORMATION & COMMUNICATION TECHNOLOGY (ICT).

(C) BUILD HUMAN CAPITAL & SOCIAL CAPITAL WHICH WILL STRENGTHEN THE "SMARTNESS" OF THE CITIES.

(D) USE OF ECOLOGICAL ENGINEERING FOR HEALING, PURIFYING & UNIFYING ALL KINDS OF EFFLUENTS OF THE CITIES.

07
Habitat

PLEASANT HABITAT

If the Six indicators of Smart City are not translated to ground; huge money will be spent in the name of Smart city which we see in hoardings, write-up, TV, Radio, discussion etc and NOT at the zero ground level. Have we the vision and commitment to make cities truly Smart? Travel every square inch of land of any city and start taking proactive actions through Town Planning Schemes under the Development Authority Act; which will make a beginning of building of Smart city. Mere vision, proposals and slogans etc will remain as such and the future generations will blame us for lack of ideas and action. We have noticed in 2015 that our thought process has become more destructive. One aspect, I would like to deal. What is happening to our Habitats? Choking, Flooding, Over-Crowding, more cars and vehicles killing people; all these mainly because of overcrowding and high rate of increasing number of cars & vehicles. City should not try to become Delhi or Bombay or Kolkata etc and commit self-suicide. City should be pleasant with evening cool breeze, without traffic hazards, zero-pollution, green city not concrete jungle, de-emphasing glamour & glitter, Violent- free and peaceful, eco-friendly with lush-green and blue water streams and rivers, more of pedestrian and cycle paths surrounded by colorful flowers and a harmonious community where each one knows each other, preservation of agricultural land and villages around the city(not encroaching agricultural land for building apartments and so called duplex units) etc. Our aim should be to make Spiritual City. It is possible with the above determinants for which it is essential to LIMIT THE POPULATION & ITS BOUNDARY. We have to stop arbitrariness and madness of limitless expansion cult. This can make Habitat a unique city. We can do it if we want to do. Develop determination and commitment to fulfill this Big Dream.

Sweet and scented breeze

Make the Habitat to laugh & enjoy And love its inhabitants

No vehicles emitting foul gases

No high rise blocks to lose identity

No concrete jungle

No network of roads dumped with cars & vehicles

To make accident and kill people

A close knitted human capital

Knowing each other intimately

Makes murder and rape etc; a thing of past

To make my Habitat a pleasant one.

08
Habitat

DEVELOPMENT-PLEDGES OF PARIS (COP-21)

The planet Earth is rushing towards creative destruction. Pledges of Paris climate change are to fulfill the "greed" of few, derailing the process of human civilization. When the humans will realize the present stage of "intellectual terrorism" as they are going against the laws of Nature? It is time to stop this "greed business" and design ways and means with positive intellect to save the humans and the earth from deadly hazards of climate change and global warming failing which the global economy is going to collapse resulting in societal disaster destroying human capital and social capital. Climate change and global warming are manmade events. We make blunders after blunders and then have Global Summit like COP21 to counteract the impacts. It is difficult to understand the logic of human species. Our actions should have been proactive so that we would have ignorant to the terms climate change and global warming.

The world is boasting of great people, great technology and everything great. But NASA has warned India about severe air pollution. Yes, this is also great. All of us will die of polluted air, but there will be no body to tell us great.

It is reported that people of China are purchasing clean air from Canada- schools are closed- Government is telling people to stay at home and not come out to roads by vehicles. ".Fresh Mountain"- the clean air from Canada people are purchasing at a rate of $28 per bottle. The cost of "premium oxygen" per bottle is $27.99. What is happening to this world is really unimaginable. Stop so called DEVELOPMENT, preserve clean air, clean water and clean land to live. India & China competing who will be NO.1 economic power. What a farce? What is this economy? People are dying by their self-deed of "making Nature nasty" and competing for what? Develop commonsense and do not make DEVELOPMENT to kill people. When good sense will prevail in humans?

With such serious crisis, we have to ensure materialization of Pledges of Paris (COP21) starting from grassroots level moving up to global level to arrest climate change and global warming knocking at our doors to take us away to a different world. Better late than never.

09

Habitat

MAKE EXISTING HABITAT SMART

All God's creation are beautiful. Why all of us in the world do not live in such environment? Is Humans have become demonic? Talk false, Fool people around you. Throw away three basics of Humanitarian quality-Truth, Order & Harmony. Try to prove right wrong things. Make promises which are not kept. People making promises are not there tomorrow. No one is accountable for the welfare of people. Laws, justice and rules are on one side; actions are just reverse. No one tolerate any one. No one has time to look to zero ground level. Policies are made in air/vacuum and time erases it all. What can we call such kind of species? Public memory is very short. A name is to be coined for such kind of species. Is our civilization is going to be Mayan?

Under such false world, we are telling people to build Smart City with investment of millions of rupees What will be approach and what they will do, perhaps any common man has no clear understanding. The word "SMART CITY" is only exciting. That is the be all and end all over our excitement. How many years it will take and how the physical, social, economic, environmental and humanitarian problems are to be solved; we do not know. Authority announcing today on the monetary requirement and ideas of smart city may not be there after sometime. Who will be accountable then? Where is the SUSTAINABILITY factor? The Smart city should have clearly spelled out the specific programs they are going to initiate with clear time limit, monetary requirement, and technology to be used and should list out benefits to be accrued to the people. Like Delhi, they should have immediately initiated one program say like restoring natural drainage channels of the city of Bhubaneswar to make the city free from water logging. No population and boundary of Smart city are fixed. There are many ifs and buts. Who listen to all these? All are busy in the present glitters and glamour of the city forgetting that how many people are dying in accidents daily, how many rapes are taking place daily, number of looting taking place daily, how many people sleep on foot path, how the life of women of the city have become unsafe and many more. City like Bhubaneswar, Comparing and competing with Delhi, Chennai etc which we say Developed Cities whereas Bhubaneswar is a developing city, is not appropriate. Babu- neta-builder nexus have killed our developed cities. They are self-centrist and hypocrite; in the name of welfare of city and such people build their own empire and fool people behind. Time has come for a change. Developed cities have become cancerous and unlivable. But good sense has prevailed- now there is an attempt to restore to its natural form. But there is still some hope left to come out of nexus and modify the mistakes. Any city, still there is hope to restore the wrongs we have committed and go ahead with full steam to make it Smart City. Although I do not have full data about Bhubaneswar, but from my day to day inter-face with the city, I can offer some suggestions as follows-

1) Fix the population of the city for all time to come.
2) Fix the boundary of the city and no change at any point of time should be made.
3) For people in general, provide adequate infrastructures and working places to fulfill their ambition so that they do not develop desire to migrate to urban area. In case more people desire to come to city build new smart city for them and do not allow them through legal means to crowd Bhubaneswar. Do not take away agricultural land for urban purpose.
4) Conceive land, air and water as one holistic unit and the make a plan to develop the smart city.
5) Full recover 10 natural drainage of the city at all cost through legal measures to check marooning of the city like Chennai.
6) Adopt ECOLOGICAL ENGINEERING for recycling of water and effective drainage and sewerage system with almost Zero maintenance cost and preserve and conserve all water bodies to make the city Green.
7) For poor people now living in slums, develop heart to provide in situ or planned rehabilitation with active participation of those people.
8) Create environment and develop effective law and order system so that the rich people put their head on their shoulders and behave like normal human beings. The present show-off business should totally stop.

9) Approach to planning and Architecture must radically change keeping in view our own culture to ensure that every square inch of land put to use without overcrowding and pollution.

10) Road side trade, commerce and business in tents should be drastically removed to provide space for pedestrians, cyclists and parking etc.

11) With only flyover, the traffic problem will not be solved. Redesign the land space basing on origin-destination survey with pedestrian and cycle paths surrounded by "Green". The P& C paths should be linked to MTS like metro and mono rail, moving roads etc. No trucks be allowed to ply on the road in the residential areas. Sand/dust movement by any means of transport should be banned. Building components factories be promoted to which dedicated roads be planned to carry sand and other building materials to totally eliminate sand/dust pollution. Noise pollution caused by any method like vehicles, DJ (**Disc Jockey**) bands etc should also be totally banned.

12) Fossil fuel vehicles/cars must be removed slowly as Delhi is doing and introduce solar and Hydrogen vehicles to keep the air fully clean. Do not increase number of cars and other fossil-fuel driven vehicles on the roads by framing regulatory measures like Singapore.

13) Develop courage not to cut a single tree in the City and devise methods how to develop without cutting trees. Germany is an example in this respect.

14) Improve the system of Health & education in the City not by building beautifully designed buildings but by filling the buildings with beautiful and dedicated faculty and man power which is more important than the beautiful buildings. Create Institutional system to develop Human Capital & Social Capital which is very essential for building Smart City.

15) Develop "green Culture" of the city not by slogan but by actually nurturing it. A tree/plant needs care and nurturing as a human baby needs. This is very important for Smart City. Make the Land, Air & Water pollution level Zero. For heaven's sake, do not cut even a single tree but make it an integral component of development like "traffic calming" etc.

16) Redesign the city in a way so that antisocial people will not get opportunity to do any kind of violence/works beyond moral norms. I am sure this can be done by space design.

17) Develop effective system to collect, transport, treat and recycle solid waste keeping in view the concept of converting "waste to wealth". From organic waste energy can be generated.

18) Apply e-governance to all kinds of activities and adopt ICT to manage various activities of the town like traffic, law & order, parking, shopping, livelihood, greenery etc.

19) In fulfilling the material needs of the people, humanitarian needs must be incorporated.

20) The Smart city design should revolve around the concept of "HEALING", "PURIFYING" & "UNIFYING". There are many more. But I think if

we start with above 20 points, making of a Smart City will start materializing and we will see a truly smart city in 10-15 years or more time. But it is time to make a beginning.

Smart, Smart and Smart

Circulated across the world

I am amazed and disgusted

As smart has become an illusion

Talks & discussions, Make it more worse

As nothing is visible as smart

We are taken for granted

And live our life as before

In as called outsmart Habitat & Culture

Suffer, Suffer & Suffer.

10
Habitat

POLUTION AND SMALL STEPS

Making existing cities as Smart cities and building New Smart cities are two challenges of 21st century. For example there is now attempt to make Delhi, a Smart City. A bold and new beginning has been made to clean Delhi Air by regulating fossil fuel driven cars and vehicle. From 01/01/2016, odd number of vehicles will run on street on odd days and even number of vehicles will run on even days. In spite of inconvenience to the commuters, CM, Delhi must be congratulated to take this innovative and dynamic decision as the first step to make Delhi, a Smart City. Welcoming this decision Rahul Bajaj said that we protect ourselves failing which we die. He is very correct, if we do not do this, people of Delhi will inhale poisonous gas and mass death will take place. There are many steps to be taken for a Smart Delhi which may take number of years. Steps are to be decided carefully to achieve the objective of Smart City. We should make Delhi free of fogs and other air pollutants and provide people pure oxygen to inhale. History tells us what happened to London in December 1952. London was vanished. Five days continuous smog blotted the Piccadilly Circus and other areas. The smog was so rough that one cannot see his own hand in front of his face. Drivers could see even less. After five days fog, thousands of people die. It is estimated that the poison cloud in London contained 2000 tonnes of Carbon dioxide,1000 tonnes of smoke particles, 370 tonnes of sulphur dioxide, 140 tonnes of hydrochloric acid and 14 tonnes of fluorine compounds. Before it happens to Delhi and other cities of India, fortunately Delhi is building the first step. It is felt that slowly and steadily Delhi should simultaneously build other steps like develop metro, mono rails, moving roads as part of MTS and link it to Pedestrian and Cycle paths, besides regulatory measures like getting license from government before purchase of fossil fuel driven cars and vehicles, paying tax to government equivalent to the cost of car etc (as in Singapore). Cost effective solar and Hydrogen driven cars should be invented for pollution-free mobility and many more ideas to be invented to make the air totally clean full of oxygen.

Similarly, the case of Waste Water management, In Odisha, India an innovative process of waste water treatment was taken up through Ecological Engineering techniques. The treatment takes place through the relationship of waste water/sewage with natural plants. For the plants the pollutants of waste water become food and they consume the pollutants and grow and the waste water is purified. No power or machinery is required. Maintenance cost is almost zero. It is extremely cost-effective and sustainable. It makes the Habitat green. But, unfortunately with time and change of government, the projects were demolished,

11
Habitat

PAST WRONG DOINGS

To create Smart Cities, we must analyze why our existing cities are so unhealthy, fit to be in ICU. Beijing chokes-206 Micrograms/cubic meter concentration of PM2.5.-, which are harmful microscopic particles that penetrate deep into lungs. This is 724% higher than WHO's recommendation PM2.5 limit of 25 Microorgrams/cubic meter. Air quality in Delhi plunged into "severe" category with PM2.5 at 197 (mc/cu.m), five times above the prescribed limits. Although data is not available, most of the Indian cities also choke. Present cities choke and maroon- with such condition we have generate new and sustainable ideas for proposed SMART CITIES. Broadly, there are six indicators to be complied with to make the cities SMART, which are- Smart living, Smart Mobility, Smart people, Smart Economy, Smart Environment and Smart Government. These six components cover up all the issues of "Environment", "Economy", and "Ecology" which are the basic foundation of cities. "Digital Infrastructure" having state-of-the art Data Center can be added being itself as a broad indicator. All city & nearby areas are badly required to be digitized so as to get advantage of GIS analysis of all spatial & non-spatial data. Even simulation of drainage of intense storm water will matter for future. We need visual &

graphic futures. Do not forget about marooned metro CHENNAI and National Capital DELHI choked with Smog and all kinds of pollution. New secured and sustainable outlook for Cities today is to predetermined population and boundary beyond which they should not be allowed to grow. It must be ensured with legal binding. If this is done, our dream of smart city perception will come true. Otherwise, same blunders will continue making life more and more miserable worst than CHENNAI & DELHI etc. For Extra population desire to stay in urban area, arrangement be made to build new towns for them. Time has come to change our mind set and radically change the concept of city building. Please let us not boast of our wrongful actions being taken for cities today because of many of us will not be there to see the consequences of our actions but our future generations are going to be suffocated. Let us not continue with slogans, publicity and self-boasting of creating organic cities but switch over to reality and then with appropriate technology generate sustainable and peaceful ideas for city building. The services of experts in the line must be utilized to rectify the past wrong doings and to develop Smart cities. It cannot be designed with only administrative service.

12
Habitat

POSITIVE INDICATORS FOR HABITATS

It is reported by some media that 10% of rich nations contributing to 90% of Carbon emission. It is in connection with COP21. How long such blame game will continue. The researchers of the University of Leicester, UK have found that Earth's oxygen level could dramatically fall due to change in Ocean temperature of just several degrees, which may likely result in the mass mortality of animals & humans. They further stated that falling oxygen level by global warming could be greater threat to survival of life than flooding. We all know nations are divided by artificial lines, but the Land, atmosphere and ocean (Water) are not divided. What devastation we see including climate change, global warming, flooding, fall in oxygen level in atmosphere, smoging of cities and all kinds land, water and air pollution are the consequences of collective impact of the responses of land, air and water holistically to the piecemeal destructive impulses of mankind in the name and for the sake of Development. What kind of development we are doing and leaving behind for our future generations where we cannot move out without putting on mask in our face and confronting always poverty, violence, terror, intolerance, petty self-interest at the cost of human interest and above all passing on "big talks" culture without ensuring that the "talks" truly benefit the humans to live a better quality of life devoid of climate change, global warming, sea level rising, flooding, atmospheric smog, and all other kinds social, economic, physical and environmental hazards and pollution. This is possible if we adopt some of the following indicators-

1) Discard use of fossil fuel energy and adopt Solar & Hydrogen energy for all human activities.
2) End the discrimination of rich and poor nations.
3) Do not talk if you can not translate it in to zero ground level.
4) Develop a sense of Enoughness by all the nations and individual citizen of the world.
5) Equal access of resources and technology for all the nations.
6) Stop playing Blame game.
7) Develop holistic understanding about Nature and its resources and forces.
8) Remember you can never win Nature, but Nature will always be victorious.
9) Change Development models which should be always in conformity with the laws of Nature.
10) Wipe out violence & terrorism for making the Development sustainable.
11) Make PEACE, the only culture of Humanity.
12) Changing Development models must incorporate "blending of science of Matter with Science of Spirituality".
13) Control population growth and more or less achieve equity in distribution of population in the land mass of the Biosphere.

14) Human Habitat planning to be designed in a holistic pattern keeping equilibrium with basic needs of humans with sustainable use of Nature's resources.

15) Ensure that Nature's resources are sustainably used, reused and recycled for any kind of Development.

16) Do not make Development whose effluent will be an overburden on earth's three landscapes.

17) Stop playing petty politics for self-interest.

18) Give top priority in building Human & Social Capital.

19) Always adopt proactive action to prevent occurrence of any physical, social, economic and environmental hazards.

20) Develop "Humanitarianism" than fanning any other "ism" for all kinds of human activities.

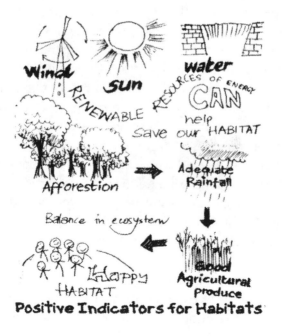

Positive Indicators for Habitats

13
Habitat

CLIMATE AND HABITAT

7 million people are drowning when climate change conference is going on at Paris-the cause of drowning is inevitably "Climate Change". Chennai one of the metros of India- will it be lost? Who is responsible for such "beyond the perception" destruction? Many opinions are emerging-" Urban Planning has failed", "Drainage and Sewerage system has failed"," the" city has grown beyond its carrying capacity", "concrete jungle gave way to violent forces of Nature" and many more. All these reasons may be true, but the origin of this disaster is "global climate change"- there is no doubt about this. Who can say that such holocaust will not drown the entire land mass of the Biosphere? The big question is the survival of humans in the planet earth. My perception of climate change is disruption of equilibrium between Natural, Domesticated and Fabricated landscapes which the Dirt in our minds blocked to conceive and implement appropriate ideas and technology to proactively develop cities and towns which are Eco-friendly, sustainable & peaceful. After appearance of Homo sapiens 1.6 million years ago, we have failed to adopt fully renewable energy resources mainly solar and Hydrogen and stressing only on economic growth depending of fossil fuel and with cut-throat competition. Top priority today is to totally

change over to Solar & Hydrogen energy from fossil fuel energy and use it in three landscapes dedicatedly especially in the Fabricated one. Till today we are allowing uncontrolled growth of population in cities and towns; the consequences of which are seen today. COP21 must continue their research on this vital issue and come up with an idea which justifies "growth in conformity with laws of Nature" failing with our hollow slogan of globalization will creatively destroy the human race. Let us not allow another "CHENNAI" to take place in any other part of the world.

The impact of climate change is clearly visible in CHENNAI, INDIA, where in winter season there is heavy downpour killing thousands of people and making life "terror-like" situation. Rains continued for long time span making life of people miserable. Report also tells us during last more than 100 years such a calamity has not occurred in CHENNAI. The leaders of COP21 must examine the causes of such horrible hazard of climate change and ignite their minds to try to find out causes and solutions of such a disaster. COP21 leaders should have made field visit of CHENNAI at least for one day to see in their own eyes how Nature becomes nasty because of human action/inaction to realize and understand the issue. It is nothing but the illogical and anti-nature consequence of the people of the globe as a whole in the name of development. If we cannot do anything then let us admit that for the sake of Development people are to be killed and we become proud of so-called development.

After COP21 can we expect climate will improve or move towards improvement as the leaders have returned to their respective countries? The people of the world are suffering because of climate change and global warming. We humbly urge upon the world leaders to tell us what to do, how to behave with the elements Nature- LAND, AIR & WATER so that every individual world citizen contributes to recovery of Nature. We will read the global deliberations on climate change, but it will be not be enough if we are not told what we will do at individual and zero ground level.

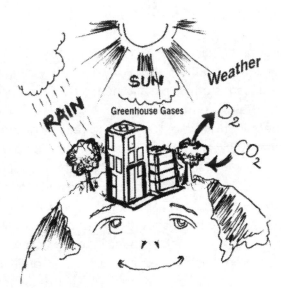

Climate and Habitat

14
Habitat

GLOBAL IMPACT ON HABITAT

In order to arrive at most appropriate deliverable solutions at grassroots level, there must be

"meeting of minds" of all world leaders. No blame game should be played. We know that the fabricated landscape of the Biosphere which consists of only 2% of total land mass of the Biosphere is mainly responsible for climate change. Besides, global warming, green house gases etc are also adversely affecting Biosphere's and human health. It is all because human unwise thoughts and actions. We are also disturbing the equilibrium of Natural, Domesticated and Fabricated landscapes for our petty interest. Fragmentation of human race sticking to their vested interest and not sharing the technology and ideas is also one of the key reasons for deterioration of the issue of climate change. We must develop "collective minds" and rise above petty self interest and share technology, ideas, resources and develop sincere desire to support other deserving countries so that collectively we can overcome the problems relating to climate change. If we can conserve and protect the natural characteristics of land, air and water and appropriate actions are taken at the grassroots level, the problem may be solved. It needs courage, conviction and commitment of the world leaders. Although the problem is highly complex, simple solutions are to be invented, which can be carried out at the field level for eliminating the risk of greatest hazard to the humanity. Failing which, the deliberations of COP21 will rot as voluminous document in the archive.

Globalization In 21st century

When I look around

Come across mere talks & promises

Experience the pinch of

Problem generating

Physical elements of habitat

More and more decay occur

With dominance of

Materialistic positivism

Taking away the

The Glamour & Glitter of

Globalization.

15
Habitat

CLIMATE HAZARDS AND HABITAT

In November 2015 the temperature is around 30 degree Celsius in this part of the world. Environmental issues started to draw attention of human species from 1950 and till 2012 more than 1159 Multilateral Environmental Agreements (MEA) has been documented. When it started in 1950, I remember the temperature was around 15 degree Celsius in the month of November in this part of the world. After 65 years the temperature has increased by about 15 degree Celsius. Thanks to the intellect of humans and 1159 MEAs. If this trend continues, the world will be burned after number of years. We cannot predict the number of years, but I hope all the scientists, leaders and people of the world have utterly failed to comply(not fight) with the laws of Nature, as a result Nature is becoming nasty to nastier. Humans have lost their heads in quest of merely economic growth through exploiting and destroying resources of our Mother planet; the consequence of which is poverty, wars, terror and all kinds of violence in social, economic and environmental sectors. The world is divided broadly into two parts –Developed & Developing. Although the Developed part is comparatively better from economic point of view, but socially and environmentally their status is declining rapidly where as in Developing part is torn between conflicts, wars, terror, poverty and all kinds of social, economic and environmental hazards. It appears both the parts are engaged in war of words through the forces of destructive petty self-interest.

Apprehending the signals of self-destruction, dialogues between countries started in 1970s and after lot of brain storming exercises, the First World Climate Conference at Geneva was organized in 1979. It was an awareness building summit about the challenges of the Environment. The World Climate Research Program was initiated and Intergovernmental Panel on Climate Change(IPCC) started its operation in 1988 to reveal scientific, technical and socioeconomic information for understanding of great risk (wipe out humans from the earth) knocking at the door of human race. Second climate change conference took place in 1990 which stressed on awareness to acceptance stage. It was evident that rapid industrialization by some nations has further deteriorated the health of the planet Mother Earth. Developing countries protested such lop sided development. Then in 1997 Kyoto Protocol emerged as part of United Nations Framework Convention on climate change (UNFCCC) with the mechanism of carbon credit system; which is termed as action stage. But countries like Japan, Russia and Canada withdrew from this protocol in 2011. There were no consensus of action of Kyoto Protocol. Since Kyoto Protocol 18 conferences of COP were held to minimize the conflicts of interest. With all such global conferences, the problem of climate change phenomena has increased. We have to wait and see the impacts of deliberations of COP 21 held at Paris.

At the grassroots level, the impact of all such global deliberations has not been felt as a result the process of climate change and global warming is further expedited. Three landscapes –Land, Air and Water have to be very carefully managed at the grassroots level. Some of the suggestions are as follows-

LAND

Three Landscapes- Natural, Domesticated and Fabricated environment must be holistically viewed. Fabricated environment (cities & towns) which covers only 2% of land mass is responsible for 75% deterioration of health of the planet earth. It implies that we do not know or we have no desire to adopt appropriate strategy to improve the health of the planet with global collective minds so that the problem of climate change and global warming is sorted out. Here the main villain is Energy. Can we totally stop use of fossil fuel energy? The people living in cities, towns and villages must switch over to renewable energy like solar, Hydrogen, Wind etc. The technology must be transferred to the poorest of the poor person so that she/he discards anything run by fossil fuel energy. The approach to planning of cities/towns must change towards more use of renewable materials and planning of habitats should provide more emphasis on pedestrian, cycle and other means through which an individual can have access to all his social, economic and environmental needs easily without going for motorized vehicles.

MTS should be the spinal cord of the city to which all other mobility modes should converge.. For doing this, all Nations of the world must unite and deliver mutual support to each other.

Tree Plantation should be taken up in a massive manner through the people living in cities/villages. Not a single tree should be allowed to be cut for any so called development work, according to which development design must be prepared.

Revival of dead soil program is initiated through 100% organic farming. Vermiculture is one of the simplest ways to achieve this. Agriculturists must be given high status in the society; providing them equal platform as given to industrialists.

Industrialization is taken up not in agricultural land but in degraded land. Technology must be available to the industry so that they do not contribute to air, water and land pollution. Techniques of converting "waste to wealth" must be invented and applied at the ground.

Steps be taken to enrich the Natural & Domesticated environment through energy and resource recycling process.

AIR

Ideas must be promoted not to disturb normal composition of air by development taken up by human species. Anything injurious to air must be discarded.

Preservation and conservation of air quality through effective and healthy management of land and water. Oxygen, Carbon dioxide and Nitrogen level in air be maintained to the extent for sustenance both biotic and abiotic communities of the biosphere.

WATER

Natural cycle of water in no case should be disturbed. Recycling of water must be taken up for all projects taken up by humans. Oceans should not be formed as a dumping yard which will affect adversely marine life forms. For example SIR11 marine life contributes to air high quantity of oxygen and once it is lost, there will be shortage of oxygen changing the climate and killing the humans. Rivers, ponds, lakes etc should not be tampered with for the sake of so called development. No pollutants like sewage and nuclear waste etc should be discharged to ocean. Ecological Engineering process should be adopted in all cases (villages & cities) to purify polluted water and then reuse and recycle which is the most cost-effective technology to purify and recycle water. Although change is difficult but this change from the routine must be adopted proactively to stop war for water. The technology establishes relationship between humans, plants, organisms, microorganisms and other elements of Nature for maintaining good health of Planet Earth. Wastage of water should be strictly prohibited by adopting different measures, besides maintaining quality of air and land.

Climate Hazards and Habitat

01
Peace

PEACE AND CIVILIZATION

The human civilization is cycle of changing events in time. From food gathers and hunters, the humans had passed innumerable stages and now presently undergoing the event of globalization. The drama of human civilization began with "individual" and "survival of the fittest" to widely varied societies sharing certain basic values such as killing is evil and certain basing institutions such as some form of family. Variety of cultures, of the people, of religious worlds, of historical traditions etc formed attitudes. Peace and violence co-exist simultaneously. Moral sense of what is right and wrong had also undergone changes in the evolution process. The history of civilization is the history of development of humanity providing broad identification of people through generations of civilizations from ancient Sumerians and Egyptians to classical and Mesoamericans to Christian and Islamic civilization and through successive manifestation of Hindu and other civilizations. The causes, emergence, rise, interaction, achievements, decline and fall of civilization determine nature, identity and dynamics of civilization.

The concept of civilized society was developed in 18th century which was opposite to Barbaric society. Civilized was good and barbaric was bad. Ideas of good and bad revolve around intellectuals, diplomatic and political powers with the beginning of 19th century. The mode of thinking in respect to values, norms, institutions, material, spiritual and culture form some kind of historical whole differentiating between "barbarism" and "civilizationism" The elements which define civilizations are broadly religion, division of people by cultural characteristics, division by physical characteristics into races, a certain degree of integration having parts related to each other. It is time to decide appropriate techniques and technology for meeting the human needs in time. This is usually known as "development" (meaning "change"), the approach of which changes with type of human associations, cultural and political entities etc. But undoubtedly religion is a central defining characteristic of civilization.

Civilizations in time have not limited identities as only religious and cultural entity, but there is shifting balance of civilizations. The oldest civilization, Indus-Valley civilization which began a "civilized world" has now practically disappeared. In the evolution process, western civilization emerged which developed interests in every other civilization and built capacity to influence the politics, economies and security of every other civilization. In general western civilization was characterized by ability to own, operate the international monetary system, becoming world's principal customer; provide the majority of the world's finished goods, domination of international capital markets, leading moral leadership and side by side massive military invention etc besides many other factors. Lessons learned from rise and fall of civilization in history are basically "dominance" and then "decline". It happened with western culture and resurgence of non-western culture began. All such rise and fall of civilizations have witnessed wars, cold-wars, war of invisible enemies simultaneously developing new ideas and technologies for the welfare of the mankind. However crisis took over all kinds of human activities including economical, political, social, urban, religion, moral, environmental, and inequity and discrimination of production and consumption as fruits of development.

Global equations are changing. Twentieth century brought about end of European dominance of global politics and economics. The present trend in the beginning of twenty-first century may witness decline of American dominance with new power axis, China-India –Brazil. The challenges of sustainable development, protecting the environment, minimizing the gap between rich and poor, reducing conflicts, initiating peace revolutions, providing food security for all, ending extreme poverty, stabilizing world population respective of development index of countries etc will be ideas dominating in the twenty-first century influencing rebalancing of economies and geo-politics. Unless these challenges are met successfully, planet earth with present 7.2 billion population producing US $60.0 trillion of output every year will be outstripped its carrying capacity creating higher degree of turbulence and conflict in all sectors of human activities. Conflicts and violence will increase between countries and haves and have not's due to dearth of life support resources like energy, water, food, air etc. There may be increasing wars in different forms between the countries for acquisition of other country resources to enhance and improve the quality of life of another country. This contradicts the concept of globalization Can it be possible to eradicate the struggle of "us" vs. "them" in the new experiment of globalization? Some of the trends like world's average economy is rapidly getting richer in terms of income per person and average income gap per person between today's richer world and developing world is narrowing slowly. Countries with survival economy are still to come out of web of poverty to be a part of globalization process. Secondly world population continues to rise to gear up growth of global economy. Production of output will be more per person by middle of twenty-first century. Total economic production is likely to be several times more than today. With higher value- addition, there will be a serious environmental crisis and ecological niches will be filled up upsetting its natural functioning. This will affect adversely both economy and ecology as a result conflicts and violence will increase to destabilize the process of globalization. Such phenomena will defeat the lifting the life style of poorest at the bottom as a result the global poverty will increase. Nearly 10 million children today die each year as the families and societies cannot sustain them. This figure may rise still higher as there is grave doubt if the present trend of globalization can cope with such serious problems. All these events will give rise to higher level of fundamentalism and radicalism as the poorest people of survival and emerging economy will be more stressed with high level of poverty, hunger and lack of access to life supporting resources like air, water and food etc. Such people if not taken care by the process of globalization will transform themselves as "terrorists" with the perception that their action is for the right cause of humanity. Some people may also join the terror group in search of purpose, excitement or status in the cadre to overcome poverty, oppression, and religious conflict etc. Terrorism in globalization era will provide oppressed people an opportunity to develop terror-psychic which will seriously affect the concept of sustainable development. Religious fundamentalism encourages radicalization to kill others although in no religion killing is justifiable and advocated. Many terrorist have repented and developed strong desire to return back to main stream of life through development. Globalization process has to take cognizance of this changing mind set and design a comprehensive package of capacity building/training to change the psychic of terrorist and bring them back to normal peaceful life. Genetic and sociobiology have advocated scientific approach to "how we stay good" and "how we turn bad". Many cases have been noticed where the terrorists have realized that they are fighting a wrong battle which is ideologically bankrupt. Such realization has transformed many terrorist to deradicalize and disengage themselves from such heinous acts. But this is not the case everywhere, as it is seen that fruits of globalization would not be divided equally among all nations as a result the phenomena of terror may continue. Some world citizens have also accused globalization of favoring richer countries by pushing up prices of their manufactured goods while reducing prices of raw materials exported by third world countries. There are varying perceptions today about globalization. One of them is based on the perception that it has potential to raise every one's living standard. But it is not happening that way, Growing inequality with advance industrialized countries also continues along with countries of emerging and survival economy. Although money flow is increasing in the developing countries, use and recycling of money have resulted in societal failures to create sustainable communities. Efficiency of governance is not improving to the scale required to make globalization work Enhancing our understanding of globalization's determinants and problems, there is need of alternative and new path which will be more responsive to people world over without any kind of discrimination. Today, basically the countries of the world have become more interdependent than ever as money, technology, raw material, finished goods, finances, ideas and cultures circulate more freely. This has given rise to international intervention in law, economics and social movements in different countries. Advances in communication through information technology and building intelligent infrastructure system with free market ideology have produced increased goods, services and capital accompanied by high rate of mobility. Movement of people and goods are facilitated by high technology modes of transport which results in open market system for free interplay of economic forces irrespective of their capacity to compete either to survive or progress or to breakdown. Such globalization of the economy need to be resisted. Instead a process of international integration of economies through restructuring of the modes of production, distribution and consumption of goods and services on a global scale without destroying existing local social structure and culture should form the cutting edge of sustainable globalization. Globalization of economy, politics, culture and technology etc is today in focus and accordingly many countries are redefining their policies and programmes. But surprisingly, human intellect has failed to realize that without "Globalization of Peace", globalization of economy, market, politics, culture, technology and law etc will threaten our very survival in the earth. Globalizing peace not only provide alternative to violence and terror but also provides opportunities to develop different processes and structural forms which will enhance human capabilities to integrate economy and technology with determinants of humanitarianism like caring and sharing, compassion, empathy, truth, order and harmony etc which will fulfill our dream of sustainable globalization. Peace will play a vital role in globalization process for emergence of a new sustainable civilization.

Peace and Civilization

02
Peace

BHUTAN AND PEACE

Kingdom of Bhutan, a small country with a population of 2.3 million is perched in the Himalayas between India and China has taught lesson to the world recently to live harmoniously and peacefully within the framework of ecology.

On March 24, 2008 the monarchy in Bhutan gave away their power to parliamentary democracy without any palpable pressure from inside or outside or any blood bath.

The party that came to power is "Peace and Prosperity Party" befitting to the ideologies adopted by successive monarchs of the Wang chuck dynasty.

This is unique in history of human civilization. The monarchy guided the country to prosperity through peace process with full dedication to environmental conservation and blending of tradition with modernity harmoniously. Development of the country is measured by GROSS HAPPINESS INDEX (GHI) and not by GNP/GDP. It is the only country in the world which has the skill of "ruling the people through peace process" for their prosperity.

The entire world and all the countries should learn the lessons of Bhutan so that Peace revolutions overtake violent revolutions in the human civilizations for safe, secured, sustainable and peaceful future of the humanity.

Salute to Bhutan
Gross happiness Index
True way of
Measuring progress of country
Products are artificial
For transitory pleasure
Can we not move away from
GDP and GNP
To live a life of Laughter, happiness & peace.

03
Peace

LEARNING THE LESSONS TO LIVE ON EARTH IN PEACE

We know how to fly on air and walk in space. We know how to dive and swim in deep water of ocean. But we do not know how to live on earth as human beings. What a paradox? Present life styles are based on the concept of "Time is Money". Every fraction of a second is spent to make life more productive and prosperous by earning more and more money setting aside all ethical/ moral/spiritual values of life. There is no doubt it is an active and dynamic life which is "individualistic- centric". Habitats are designed devoid of value system where the humans are stressed and tortured.

The western world is more productive and prosperous but it has been admitted by the people of such part of world that they have lost peace in the society, their inner peace and mental peace. In some other parts of the world, people are less active, productive and prosperous but are relatively peaceful and happy. Thus there is relative peace with less action and prosperity and on the other side there is absence of peace with abundance of prosperity. It is now a challenge for the humanity to provide prosperity for ALL with Peace. In order to achieve this life style, we have to think and initiate actions at global as well as local levels to learn new lessons of Habitat design.

At the global level we have to change our mindset from "Time is money" to "Time is Art" accepting the aboriginal meaning of time as healing, purifying and unifying. The humanity has to realize that time is infinity moving energy which determines the "When's" of bad or good times. This calls for global recognition of "Science of spirituality" and its development for application by each and every world citizen in their professional and personal activities. "Science of matter" is already developed to a great extent, through which we are deriving prosperity without peace.

"Ultimate reality" of life is Peace, which is a powerful energy to redirect all kinds of constructive human activities. Recognizing "Science of spirituality" and developing it as a systematic knowledge that explains the meaning and purpose of existence in the world, is the challenge before the mankind. Spirit is a conscious energy and science of spirituality deals with such conscious energy. The habitat /abode of conscious energy is the human body and body of all other life forms. The body consists of matter which is only activated through transmission of "Conscious Energy" into it from the prime source Absolute Energy of Consciousness. The media of transmission is the spiritual waves of universe like the waves of ocean we see. But the wave of universe is not visible to our naked eyes, like the electro-magnetic waves.

The conscious energy enables all life forms to make five sensory instruments of body (matter) operational and active, with which we physically move our all parts of the body, think, act, decide and take all other actions. The most important function of conscious energy is generation of thoughts from the minds, which will in turn empower every individual to think for himself, not in an individualistic – centric manner but as a fraction of universal conscious energy (Absolute Energy) to realize quintessence of life. It is up to each individual to determine to what extent and how to use this empowerment of conscious spirit to live on earth.

Start with the study of the world, the individual life and relationship between them. The outcome of the study ultimately will lead us to the concept of the blending of the science of matter with science of spirituality which will endow the humanity with the principles of right living on the Earth.

At local/individual level, character of action is to be changed from selfishness to selfless service adopting the basic principles of spirituality which are healing, purifying and unifying. This will result in change of mind set from "only self prosperity" to "prosperity for all". This requires enrichment of inner space of every individual to increase more and more positively charged "conscious energy". Consciousness is to conditioned to blend right proportion of matter and spirit to provide prosperity for ALL with Peace. Negatively charged conscious energy results in destruction like terrorism etc whereas positively charged conscious energy leads to Peace and Happiness. At the individual level this is to be learned for self - realization and a self-realize person sees himself as a part of positively charged universal conscious energy. Once this is achieved, the lessons of living on earth are well defined, basing on which thoughts are reformed towards unification of values with actions.

Educating each individual accordingly, absolute peace and bliss become a beacon for the rest of the world to follow and steer their lives towards peaceful evolution by developing the principles of "Mutuality" and truly establishing peaceful connectivity with other human beings. Thus key lessons to be learned by each and every world citizen to live on earth peacefully are an integrated package of action linked to wisdom, true knowledge and self-realization establishing connectivity of his conscious energy with the Absolute Energy of Consciousness. Then only prosperity with peace will prevail on Mother Earth.

Peace & Management

Management has become a productive faculty, being applied to almost all the professions in the world. Delivering goods and services with the processing of resources in a most effective manner is the basic strategic growth of management. Management ideas are organized in all sectors of human activities ranging from the needs to fulfill basic survival requirements of humans to high-tech career options like probing space computer, telecommunication, nuclear energy, genetics and all other professions. Today management education is incomplete without understanding the basics of value-based approach, systematic way of looking at the processes, career opportunities etc for promoting a high level of prosperity of mankind with peace.

But unfortunately all kinds of management professions have failed to provide the necessities of "ultimate reality" of life – a violent free healthy peaceful life to each and every member of global human family without discrimination with genuine (not virtual) happiness from the sustainable and productive use of both human and natural capital of the biosphere. The achievement of ultimate reality of life is the greatest challenge for the profession of "Management", for the survival of mankind in the world.

What kind of management faculty need to be developed to achieve this? The only answer is to make the right and most appropriate choice of profession which can only be termed as "Peace Management". The profession of Peace Management will have the critical responsibility to empower all other professions of today's world to incorporate peace as an input. This will enable all the professions to design techniques and operations to provide security like food, shelter, social, economic and environmental needs.

Sustainable prosperity with peace for All without any discrimination will be the final product of "Peace Management" profession. This calls for innovative idea generation to design, operate and improve the systems as well as human psychic that create products and services which should be economically viable (adopting the principles of eco-economy), socially satisfying, politically humanitarian, technologically efficient, environmentally sustainable and morally sound to meet the real (not virtual) needs of sustainable prosperity with peace.

This will create a new trend befitting to the challenge of curbing the present ills and violence of global human society. This will be an exciting and a positive career option to discover unexplored territory of growth and development management. Apart from being lucrative, this new field of Peace Management will require high level of specialization. It will open up new vistas to the delight of students providing them with wider horizon of holistic knowledge bringing about the component of "peace" in their respective professions which will ultimately result in sustainable peaceful benefits to the humans in all their pursuits. Today's youths have to come out of age old traditional management career options and should be ready to take a plunge into the new creative field of Peace Management.

It is a challenge for all management schools and institutes of the world to start "Peace Management" course to create productive brand managers of Peace who will be empowered to reverse the present violent process and create different types of peaceful transformation processes categorized as physical (as in manufacturing), location (as in transportation and habitats), social (as in healing, purifying and unifying the people), exchange (as in retailing), storage(as in warehousing), physiological (as in health care), psychological(as in mental and psychic care), environmental(as in eco-system care) and informational (as in telecommunication, computer and other information technologies) etc.

Let the top management schools of the world think seriously to initiate this new and innovative profession of "Peace Management" which in future will emerge as the most preferred career options to benefit the humanity.

POLITICAL PARTIES AND GOVERNMENTS – PEACE, VIOLENCE AND PROSPERITY.

Today in 193 countries of the world there are innumerable numbers of political ideologies as well as political parties. Every country has a specific system of government ruling the people. The political ideologies are in the process of evolution and also changing at a faster rate. With globalization process, there is now more flux in political ideologies and governments.

Each and every political party or even dictators/ monarchies /military rules have two basic responsibilities to discharge namely welfare of the people and protecting the territories of the country. In the present world "Democracy" is normally accepted as best form of government.

Today when we analyze the literatures of politics and governments, generally the geopolitical condition is conceived as empowering people to control their own food, water, shelter, and energy with access to global economy, technology and protection. All these would be realized if the societies are structured primarily as a fabric of locally sustainable inputs having global access to information. Marketable commodities to facilitate involvement in a global economy tie to a larger political and technical entities is the need of the day.. Many prosperous countries of the world have supposed to achieve all these conditions. But still in those countries there are unrest, conflicts, absence of psychic –gratification and peacelessness; rather the people of many such countries are desperate with health, environment and problems relating to violence /conflicts in spite of their very high level of materialistic affluence. Besides, the poorer and developing countries are becoming more and more victims of anti-welfarism and violence.

All such ground reality check makes me and all world citizens to think and realize that there is some basic element is missing in all the political ideologies, parties and governments ruling us. The missing link is lack of understanding of ultimate reality of life which is only PEACE AND NOTHING BUT PEACE. It is not that the present world is not talking or acting on peace. The world as a whole with all kinds of ideologies and governments are deliberating on peace in a lop-sided manner without being serious or ignorant to incorporate peace as an instrument in welfare programs of the mankind.

The UN talks today more of peace as if it is only capable of bringing world peace. But unless all the world citizens express concern and take responsibility for peace building activity, peace will be eluding for all time to come in human civilization. UN being apex global organization for peace, it must work out strategy to empower and motivate each and every world citizen in the peace building process instead of trying and acting alone for peace; which will not be successful at any point of time today or in future.

In 1992 UN Secretary General Boutros Boutros Ghalis launched "An agenda of peace" – introduce a vision in which tools like preventive diplomacy, peacemaking, peace keeping and peace building were brought formally into UN's lexicon, with the objective to initiate effective and timely steps to secure lasting peace.

From 1992 -2007 what happened to this UN's Agenda for Peace? Peace, for which it is almost mandatory to include human nature through humanitarian actions was ignored with overriding political actions. Between 1995-2000, the UN continued to search for more effective ways to respond to political complexities and humanitarian consequence of such crisis to give reality to the Agenda for Peace.

Thus the political effort to bring peace, the human rights attempt to prevent impunity and humanitarian effort to save lives should be managed in harmony. In order to achieve this, all political parties of the world must adopt the concept of convergence of political efforts with humanitarianism so that there is effective management of humanized politics with more humanitarian activities. Why the UN or the human society globally is not able to do it?

The crux of the problem is our lack of proper understanding of peace. Peace, that we talk of today has ignored human nature which includes both rulers (politics, political parties and governments) and the ruled (common world citizens). Irrespective political ideologies, it is observed that day by day the basic source of political struggle among those competing for control and ruling of the populace is becoming more violent and complex.

It appears that this inter and intra conflicts in the politics and politicians have created radical groups (like terrorists) to support people struggling for control of their own lives and destinies. This is a dangerous trend of failure of politics, politicians and governments who are more interested for their vested interest than the sustainable welfare of the people as a whole.

The leaders of political parties who are supposed to maintain moral character and integrity are victims to the most aggressive ways of ruling the people taking advantage of weakness of ideologies, religion, cast, creed and color line etc. Thus there is now urgent need to reinvent peace –centric political ideologies and political leaders to design a consensus strategy to understand the basics of peace and actions to be taken to translate the ideas to grassroots level so that peace prevails from grassroots to global levels.

Peace is perceived now and theorized as subjective and it is normally accepted as "calmness" after war, violence, conflict etc. No one including UN perhaps is serious for developing the concept of "objective sustainable peace". The humanity must now accept Peace as objective and develop ideas to make it sustainable for implementation.

This needs developing and strengthening of structural linkages between humanitarian and peace operations. In addition, several other dimensions like military, eco-economic, improving the functioning of the human minds; human rights etc are to be fitted into holistic dimension of sustainable peace.

It is accepted today that democracy – a political philosophy is the best instrument to govern the people for prosperity and peace. But in many countries, democracy is transformed to mobocracy and or emergency is imposed for dictatorship/ military rule. In mobocracy instead of "law of rule", "law of jungle" operates.

The reactions to such political activities and the governments lead to conditions which threaten peace. In other forms of government the situations are still worst. Thus there is now urgent need to reinvent and rewrite the concept of peace for the humanity with the dimension of objectiveness and sustainability.

Politics, political parties and governments have to be reformed to redesign their structures and to take another look to wisdom of peace so that people living any part of the world enjoy prosperity with happiness and peace. They have to modify their thoughts and actions in the Global village of today with its borderless trading regime. Understanding and applying law of Nature of the biosphere to the political ideologies and governments need to recast our mindsets because the parameters what we must do, have changed.

Political Parties and Governments - Peace, Violence and Prosperity

06

Peace

Peace Education

Peace education as a first step towards sustainable peace culture must be introduced which refers to a more holistic framework of consciousness – raising for learning the lessons of development issues to design programs to resolve problems of militarization, human right abuse, cultural conflicts, environment destructions, personal security, Habitat security & peace and inner peace etc. Peace education must be started from the nursery to highest level of faculties. Peace education must be from womb to tomb to make the world vibrant with happiness and peace.

Ministry/Department of Peace should be established by each country, the guidelines and the principles of which should percolate to grassroots level through well designed political and governmental structures and channels. It is to be ensured that "Peace" is an input to all kinds of development programs to responsibly fulfill the needs of the people in a sustainable manner.

Some of the issues like reduction of conflict due to competition for global resources, elevation of environmental status and care, changing consumption pattern with a sense of enoughness, reduction of demands upon state and federal resources, reduction of the adverse effects of external political and economic changes, priorities and strategies addressing to social, economic, political demand, convergence of "science of spirituality" and "science of matter" etc are to be resolved both at the micro and macro level of the individual/ community/ society/ country and the world as a whole. All such issues to a great extent are dependent on psychic powers of individuals, which are real. The government uses psychics and remote views, the CIA uses them and the FBI has been known to crack cases with the help of psychics. Psychic powers do in-fact exists and we all have the ability to develop them. First one must be in the right mind frame to learn. The conscious mind has to be linked with the subconscious / unconscious mind to lead.

Mastering the brain frequencies to separate conscious thoughts from subconscious /unconscious thoughts is the hardest task to be achieved. Once this is achieved, one is the right mind frame to acquire the thought of "nothingness". When one thinks of nothing, psychic notions come from unexplained sources, not from brain leading thoughts.

07
Peace

PRELUDE TO NATURE'S FURY AND HUMAN VIOLENCE

What we see today across the world is a prelude to Nature's fury and human violence. Humans are today blindfolded, not able to conceive "timelessness" of time as a result all their thoughts and actions are misdirected and destructive. Politicians do not see anything beyond political gimmicks. Scientists do not see beyond science. Economists, Sociologists, Engineers and Technologists, Environmentalists and all other professionals engaged in their respective professions have developed outlook not to see anything beyond their fragmented boarders. Every one opposes every one for the sake limited vested interest forgetting and ignoring the basic truth of "Holisticness" of one human global family. Sickness and divisibility of one member of family is the beginning of a serious kind of tragedy for the family as a whole.

In addition, the humans are becoming more and more hostile towards Mother Nature, of whose we are the offspring/products. Tolerance capacity of Mother Nature needs to be realized. Mother's dream is always for welfare, prosperity and PEACE of her children. But if the children are led astray beyond a limit, Mother can be as nastier as possible. This is happening today?

Mother and children relationship is a bridge of love, affection, empathy, caring and sharing and above all PEACE. However, the children of Mother Nature are becoming naughtier and naughtier day-by-day as a result a crack has appeared in the bridge of relationship which is widening at a rapid rate as is evident from the recent events like earthquake in Haiti, China and eruption of volcanic ash in Iceland etc.

The earthquake in China on 14 April 2010 killed more than 600 people and injured thousands. On the same day in seven districts of India in Bihar, West Bengal and Assam, a severe wind speed of 120km per hour left 120 people dead and hundreds injured. Further on the same day, hundreds of people of Iceland's have fled rising floodwaters as high as 10 feet since the volcano under a glacier erupted. The water could chill the lava causing it to fragments of glass. Such calamity may also lead to weather change. Many such things are happening daily around the worlds which are not reported. The forecast is much more; yet to come. Besides earthquakes etc, Tsunami, flood, tornado, sea swallowing land and above all astronomical disaster which may wipe out earth-like planets in the system either absorbing them into massive planets known as hot Jupiter's(as they orbit closer to their suns) into their own mass or sling-shotting them into the far reaches of solar system.

The cardinal principle of evolution-generation, operation and dissolution is to continue for eternity.

But unfortunately due to human thought and action, the dissolution process is expedited. State of the planet earth is well known now, which is in the last cancerous stage. But humans as a whole are least concerned and keeping their operational activities in a creatively destructive manner which give rise to violence not only among themselves but also with Mother Nature who is reprimanding erring humans with all sorts of its destructive tools. If we ignore the present happenings, which are prelude to mass destruction, then anything may happen to wipe out humans from the world. We must widen our minds and five sensory instruments to listen to the urgent call of SOS nature and act immediately, so that the earth as well as the humans are saved.

THE ONLY ANSWER TO ALL THE ILLS WE EXPERIENCE TODAY IS TO ADOPT A PEACE CULTURE THROUGH PROMULUGATION OF PEACE AND ITS TECHNOLOGY IN EVERY SPHERE OF HUMAN ACTIVITIES AND PRESSURE SHOULD BE PUT UPON UN TO ADOPT 13 MOON 28 DAYS CIVIL PEACE TIMECALENDAR AS SOON AS POSSIBLE FOR CHANGING OF HUMAN MIND SET FROM VIOLENCE TO PEACE.

Prelude to Nature's Fury and Human Violence

08
Peace

JUSTICE & PEACE

Justice is truth, order and harmony in action. Truth is that which never changes over time. It is eternal in nature. Order is the logical sequential steps to assess and achieve righteousness. Harmony in essence symbolizes "similarity" and "empathy" to build peaceful relationship between objects and environment both in biotic and abiotic world.

Justice is also concerned with moral standards with regards to behavior, more responsibility referring to our conscience - a field of energy generated by the Absolute Energy of Consciousness and moral identity differentiating between right and wrong, which includes ethics, principles, non-violence and goodness etc.

Justice can be perceived also as distinct from, and more important than, benevolence, charity, mercy, generosity or compassion. All these attributes are valuable, but it is not right to place them over justice. The origin of justice needs to be explored from the "science of spirituality" – a supreme form of energy that ignites for sustenance of both biotic and abiotic world.

From this highest form of energy, justice trickles down to individual, family, community, society, nation, inter-nation, global and universal entities. It can also be perceived as divine command. Divinity is usually linked to our faith of God. But if we apply reason and science to divinity, it is transformed to Absolute Energy of Consciousness which determines universalistic justice providing approach and solution to the members of human family to live a life enriched with "justness" leading to peace.

We are more concerned to develop a true culture of justice to humans regardless of diversity of culture, race, gender, religion, nationality and all other features to maintain peaceful "oneness" of human family without any discrimination.

In general parlance, theories of distributive and retributive justice to great extent contribute to peace. The distributive justice deals with the type and Nature goods to be distributed (is it to be wealth, power, respect and / or some combination of these things?) - Between what entities are they distributed? Humans, sentient beings, the members of single human society / nations need to be provided with proper justice with equal distribution (equal, meritocratic according to social status and or according to need?) Humans answer to these questions varies from time to time of human civilization. For example today 1.1 billion people constituting 18 percent of total world's population live below World's Bank $2 per day poverty line. Is this fulfills the objective of distributive justice? Distribution of goods equally, satisfying the basic needs of people as what they need as well as they deserve, fairness in distribution of two kinds of goods (a) liberties (b) social and economic goods, just acquisition of and transfer of distribution of goods and welfare – maximization, and human rights etc are some of the criteria to fulfill requirement of justice to maximize welfare across all individuals.

The theories of retributive justice are concerned with punishment for wrong doing and also provide answer to (a) why punish (b) who should be punished (c) what punishment should be awarded?. Although punishment is a bad treatment, it is necessary to maximize the overall good in the long term in mainly three ways (a) deterrence – punishment might lead people to make different choices to maximize welfare (b) rehabilitation – to make bad people to better ones (c) security – limiting the opportunity of bad people by capital punishment /imprisonment etc to cause harm to others. In an imperfect world, institutions of justice are required to instantiate ideals of justice; if not with full perfection but nearing perfection.

Justice can only empower peace if its basic role of delivery of truth, order and harmony from individual to global level is responsibly discharged. Innocent people should not be the victims and scarified at the altar of justice in a falsified manner. This will to a great extent contribute to prevalence of sustainable peace of the humanity and the biosphere.

Peace & Justice

Two sides of one coin

Justice contributes to peace

The way to justice is

Through healing, purifying and unifying

Let the human mind adopt

The three commandments

To fill the world with

With the fragrance of justice & Peace.

09
Peace

BIOSPHERE PEACE MOVEMENT (BPM)

Will the present approach and ideas deliberated from Kyoto Protocol (which expired in 2012) to Bali summit (December 2 -14, 2007) and COP21, Paris provide and improve comfort level of climate for humans globally? It is a big and complex question to be answered. We are only buying time and shouting from the top of the roof that "No time left, unless we act now and cut emission by half" After Kyoto, similar types of announcements were made, but the climate change issue is further deteriorating. The outcomes of Global summits, conventions, conference and workshops have only able to pile up documents after documents without any positive action or impact on this critical issue at the grassroots level.

It seems human ideas and intelligence has narrowed down to build more and more statistics on climate change in a fragmented manner. If we do not enlarge and expand our mind power to "holistic intelligence", many more summits in future will be organized which will have hardly any positive impact on climate change.

I strongly argue that the issue of climate change can only be tackled if we make an attempt to understand the evolutionary forces of the universe, the planet earth (lithosphere, atmosphere and hydrosphere) and the human interventions having impact on climate change. Universe is still continuing as its galaxies, stars, sun and solar system, moon, constellations, comets and meteorites and planet earth are woven into an entity of "wholeness" bonded and sustained by various sources of energy from which different kinds of forces are emerging. The solar system is an extremely crucial part of the universe. Planet earth is unique as it supports life. The "wholeness" characteristic of the universe will be transformed to "nothingness", if anyone member of the "woven entity" especially that of the solar system is detached from the web. It is acknowledged today that the earth is dying; as a result there is inevitable human suffering and threat of species extinction and transformation of universe to nothingness. Climate variability and climate change expedite the dying process of the earth.

Study of literature of climate change highlights that climate fluctuation arises because of changes in earth's orbit, to solar radiation, to the positions of the continents and to concentrations of atmospheric greenhouse gases. Some of the main findings of this study are that the 20th century was the warmest of the past 1000 years, 1990s were the warmest decades of the millennium in the northern hemisphere and 1998 was the warmest year. It is said that increase of greenhouse gases is the main factor contributing to global warming in the late 20th century.

In order to enable the humanity to control and regulate climate change in a positive manner, it may be useful to know the climate throughout the history. In the past 120 million years, the Cretaceous period (120-65 million years ago) was 5-7degree Celsius warmer than the present and carbon dioxide concentrations were much higher than today. During the Tertiary period to the Quaternary period (2.5 million years ago) cooling took place and climate was influenced by the location and configuration of continents, presence or absence of ice sheets, changes to the earth's orbit that affected radiation received from the sun and high greenhouse gas concentration. Past about one million year was characterized by a series of changes from ice age (glacial periods) to interglacial period. Other variations in earth's lithosphere, hydrosphere and atmosphere took place during last forty thousand years to twenty thousand years.

All these coincide with variations in earth's orbit that affect the amount of distribution of solar radiation reaching the earth. Variation of earth's orbit is not influenced by the role played by lithosphere, hydrosphere and atmosphere but also by in explainable natural changes of constituents of universe especially the negative human interventions.

Perhaps, the hypothesis that earlier many universes have appeared and dissolved and present universe is the recreation after dissolution of previous universe is to be accepted as creation, dissolution and recreation as the natural law of universe. Life forms on earth especially perhaps the most intelligent species, the humans have extremely crucial role to play to prolong the life of the present earth / universe through creative constructions or expedite the dissolution process by creative destructions.

This implies that the humans must develop their intelligence to think and act holistically considering all the natural functioning of the parts of the earth and the universe, simultaneously ensuring that their activities / interventions not only decrease the harmful level of concentration of greenhouse gases, but regulate and limit the earth's /universe's natural destructive forces through initiation of proactive earth-universe friendly actions. Only with such holistic approach, we can save the earth from dying and regulate the climate change to our advantage, simultaneously increasing the life span of the earth/universe.

Since 19th century, greenhouse gas problem has been accelerated. Side by side the humans are trying to develop their knowledge and intelligence to counter the destructive impact by deliberating ideas in summits like Kyoto, Bali and other macro and micro level interactions. But unfortunately the recommendations of such summits and interactions are not translated into action at the field level.

We have gathered huge amount of information and statistics on climate change phenomena along with recommendation to cut the emission level only but unable to establish guidelines /solutions to other determinants like variation of earth's orbit, reasons for natural changes of warming and cooling etc.

I do not like to further elaborate on increasing emission rate of greenhouse gases and on the recommendations of summits like Kyoto, Bali etc as they are well known to all world citizens.

Till December16, 2007 Bali climate deal was facing rough weather as US voicing "serious concerns" over its provisions and complaining that it did not do enough to commit countries like India and China to big cuts in greenhouse gas emissions. However, ultimately a "road map" was agreed tentatively in Bali which implies that a new climate treaty must be negotiated by end of 2009 to replace Kyoto treaty. But this did not happen.

The voices of the developing countries were considered and incorporated in the recommendations of Bali summit. The new agreement will mean (a) a new climate treaty must be negotiated by 2009to replace the Kyoto treaty (b) the treaty, to come into force in 2012, also sets of a global agreement to stop tropical deforestation. (c) Instead of requiring the developed nations to cut emissions by 24 to 40 percent by 2020, the road map now says countries recognize that deep cuts in global emission will be required. Let us wait and see how the final recommendations of Bali summit are translated into action by different countries to minimize adverse impact of climate change. There must be meeting of the minds between developed and developing countries with respect to mainly two key points (a) making available of technologies by the developed countries to developing countries (b) reducing the emission rate in developed countries and permitting the emission rate of developing countries to a level without compromising their growth of economy for prosperity with peace.

> **God bless the Biosphere**
>
> **The space that I love**
>
> **Sustains me**
>
> **And sustains all life forms**
>
> **To keep the Biosphere living**
>
> **Let the mind set of humans**
>
> **Change**
>
> **To the culture of**
>
> **Truth, Order & Harmony**
>
> **To keep the Biosphere living.**

10
Peace

RELEVANCE OF IDEA OF "SUCCESS OF PEACE" IN TODAY'S TECHNOLOGICALLY COMPLEX WIRED WORLD.

Swami Vivekananda said "Take up an idea. Make that idea your life-think of it, dream of it, and live on idea. Let the brain, muscle, nerves, every part of your body, be full of that idea, and just leave every other idea alone. This is the way to success." In today's complex world "success" is the key word. Everyone needs it. Success in economy, technology, business, industry, IT sector, diplomacy, politics, academics and all other human endeavors (all components of "Matter" only) is the focus today. To a great extent, success has been achieved in different sectors, but unfortunately it is not "inclusive" and linked to "Spirituality-Consciousness-Peace", as a result we find as result we find increasing violence, discrimination, inequity and stratification of human society which to a great extent has affected the normal functioning of Biosphere and the life-support system. Success is an "IDEA", but the success we are proud of today's world seems to be virtual and is not sustainable. This is because the real and sustainable idea is not built into the "success idea". Today, the humanity is advocating and trying to promote sustainable development, ignoring the basic concept that "sustainable development and Peace will rise and fall together". All successes will be transformed to failures if the idea of "success of Peace" is not blended to "success of Matter". This can only happen if the humans will chain their ego and unchain their spirit with the realization that success of today is giving rise to violence and all kinds of social, economic, and environmental meltdown including loss of basic humanitarian qualities at individual, family, community, social, national, international and global level. For example Phillips Centre for Health and Wellbeing, Amsterdam has come out with a research finding that "35 is the new 40 as Americans feel the pressures of middle age earlier than ever". This is now happening all over the world due to pressure of unsustainable globalization delinked from peace. Once the mankind is able to unchain their Spirit, they will be able realize the relevance of SCIENCE of "Spirituality-Consciousness-Peace" which needs to be blended with "Science of Matter" for a peaceful and sustainable future of human civilization. A total reform is needed in human thought, emotion and action to adopt this Idea so that "JUSTICE" is delivered to Biosphere. Time is highly ripe now to measure development in terms of "Global Peace PRODUCT" (GPP) and "Global Environment Product" (GEP) instead of GDP/GNP. This is the KEY IDEA of today- a challenge to be met at any cost to ensure that the humans are not wiped out from the universe.

11
Peace

PEACE CALENDAR – 13 MOON 28 DAYS A PERFECT HARMONY OF TIME

Like space, whose measurement has been standardized, it is extremely urgent to standardize time measurement basing on the laws of nature. The time is infinity and the time calendar design should produce faculties to create events to be operated especially by the humans, which should be regular, harmonious and peaceful in nature.

This will reconstruct our psychic through infusion of orderly and harmonious impulses into our minds so that all the responses are peaceful in order to enable "Peace" to rule our planet and the universe. Since appearance of Homo sapiens, they have adopted different types of calendar in the process of evolution.

Perhaps, the Gaulish Coligny calendar is the oldest celetic solar/lunar calendar, which tried to reconcile both cycles of the moon and sun. But the phases of the moon were given more importance, as each month always begins with the same moon phase. The mathematical calculations made it normal 12 months calendar in sync with moon and the whole system was kept in sync by adding an extra month every two and half years. Besides there were also Mediaeval Irish and Welsh, Pre-celetic, Neolithic, Neopagan calendars etc adopted from time to time.

Before 1582, 28 days 13 moon calendar system was in force which Pope Gregory XIII revised it in 1582 to 12 months calendar basing on the natural cycle of the solar year, where its months are of unequal length. The Gregorian calendar continuing till date divides the year as if it were a 2-D circle, 360 degrees of the circle is divided into 12 subsections of 30 degrees each, making a month of 30 days. This results in 12 x 30 = 360 days leaving 5 extra days. To adjust these 5 extra days, months were made irregular with 31, 30,28 days and every 4th year one day is added in the month of February making it 29 days in place of 28 days. The 12 months correspondent to 12 hours: 60 minutes clock, usually known as 12:60 timing frequency.

This is a flat and irregular measure of time and not correlated to nature's cycles of time. This time measurement distorts our minds towards a disharmonious and incoherent violent world. The distortion of minds exposed our central nervous system to artificial rhythm of the clock and 12 months calendar, as a result our physical – mental – emotional body is delinked from natural cycle and oriented towards a mechanistic structure dominated by "matter".

Such an artificial calendar drifts away the humanity from truth, order and harmony contributing to acceleration of violent thoughts and actions. The resultant effects of such drifting are more organized crimes, wars, diseases, failure of criminal justice, mafia culture, forgery, espionages, dirty businesses, unhealthy and unethical competition between industries and farm activities, money laundering and terrorism etc. Secret weapons for the wars of the future are constantly surfacing. Curtain is slowly rising for high technology wars with lasers, chemicals, microwave radiations, and germ etc. A recent media report has exposed that since 2001 till date the USA has spent $44.00 billion in germ warfare research. All these go to prove the perversion of scientific ingenuity – a serious consequence of continuance of violent calendar diverging more and more science of matter and science of spirit at a faster rate of time. Such effects have given rise to a "apocalyptic cult" who believe that the "end of world" is approaching fast for which they are prepared to voluntarily give their lives to delay the doomsday.

In order to counteract all such "creative destruction" and to put a stop to activities of a number of radical groups like apocalyptic sects etc, we have to find answers to the pressing question of human existence and our future of earth. The answer is reversal from our present violent path of thought and action to a path of peace and harmony with nature, enriching self-knowledge (exploring 'I' and its eternal connectivity with "matter" and "spirit" and an expanded consciousness). The first crucial task is to reverse the path in the process of time infinity for readoption of "Peace Calendar" – the 28 days

13 moon calendar which was followed over 5500 years before the Gregorian calendar came into force.

Peace being the nature of the universe, adoption of Peace calendar will begin to synchronize with laws of nature thereby promoting harmony and balance in intra and inter – human relationship with the biotic and abiotic world of the planet earth/universe. In the beginning of the 21st century and new millennium, there is urgent need to adopt harmonious and orderly measurement of time so that it will invoke constructive inner harmony and consciousness to rule our activities to mould both the inner and outer world for transformation into an entity of sustainable peace.

This will encompass movement of planetary objects like stars, moons and planets etc as reference points eternally linked to nature of time, so that mankind psychic, thoughts and actions are the outcome of balanced blending of proportion of science of matter and science of spirit. This will generate radiant constructive energy which will drive all social, economic, political, environmental and technological activities of human race to develop a culture of peace. The Peace calendar is a 28 days 13 moon calendar. The year has been divided by nature in 13 months as moon completes one orbit around the earth in 364 days and every moon of 28 days is equal to every other moon.

Thus there is a harmonic standard of 13 moons 28 days maintaining 52 weeks with 7 days in a week. This result in making every day of the week and day of moon same for each and every one of 13 moons. The first day of every year and every moon is Sunday. Every month end is Saturday. Day/date of every month will be uniform. This calendar reflects perfect periodicity as every one time we go around the sun, the moon goes around earth 13 times. There is one day gap between earth movement around the sun and moon's movement around the earth. This one day is a "day out of time bound" and is to be celebrated by one human family living in different parts of the earth as the "World Peace Day". Peace is infinite, so the time and human mind. "Infinity – time -mind– peace" is a holistic concept for which a perfect calendar needs to be designed as a regular and harmonious calendar. Peace calendar of 13 months 28 days fits perfectly to the concept, which makes the human mind peaceful. With mind at peace and mind over matter, universal spirit prevails. According to this calendar July 26 which is the first magnetic moon day is the New Year Day of the Peace calendar. The Peace Calendar ends on July 24 after the moon completes one orbit around the earth in 364 days. Further there is now leap year occurring every 4 Gregorian years.

This is solved in the Peace Calendar by accumulating 13 days every 52 years, which is the term of the solar-galactic cycle. These thirteen –days-out-of time is to be organized as Jubilee celebration every 52 years. This festival will be a grand one to be celebrated by the humanity world over for ushering and era of Peace through culture. Culture of time will converge with culture of mind and peace. The calendar will serve as a holistic tool to produce harmony and order in our life's cycle process. According to Dr. Jose Arguelles, PhD "The simple and easiest way to reprogram your daily awareness of actual awareness of time is to follow 13 moon calendars". Mahatma Gandhi had also said "I have been informed of, and I welcome, the international movement for calendar reform..... I am always ready to endorse any honest movement which will help to unify the people of the world".

In order to have universal acceptance of 28 days 13 moon calendar, Planet Art Network (PAN) Nodes have been established in over 90 countries of the world. The meaning of ART in its aboriginal sense is understood as healing, purifying and unifying and bringing people together into coherent purposive groups. As such PAN engages in Art, Science, and Spirituality furthering the evolution process of humanity in harmony with biosphere. This in essence, converges science of matter with science of spirituality which I termed it as "Peace Technology".

12
Peace

HAPPINESS AND PEACE FOR SOCIAL ORDER

Happiness is one of the components of "Matter" of Peace, besides security and comfort. True happiness is a stepping stone to peace- the ultimate reality of life. It revolves around the concept of "Utilitarianism" and "fundamental Moral values" of human action. The theory of Utilitarianism, the supreme good is the greatest happiness of greatest number is gradually becoming invalid. It is well known today that the richest man of the world may not be the happiest one. Desire is the crucial determinant of happiness. We have to differentiate between happiness and pleasure. Pleasure is short term where as happiness is for a longer time. Acquisition of material goods normally leads to pleasure, which some time we confuse with happiness. A good ratio between "satisfaction of desires" and "total number of desires" is also perceived as happiness. Desires are unlimited in the utilitarian concept. Limiting desires and making an effort to fulfill limited desires within the framework of whole world of desire, purpose, morality, education, positivity and ethical institutional life and social order may lead to some degree of happiness. Increasing and limitless desires perhaps may yield more pain than happiness/

pleasure. It is time now to adopt with consensus that only acquisition of more and more goods of matter de linking from all other aspects of life will not bring happiness.

Happiness consists in the aggregate of all "matter" and "antimatter" goods properly ordered. A child symbolizes perfect entity of happiness from the stage of his birth till the time of interface with "matter goods." Till this time, there is no desire in the body-mind entity of the baby but all the needs both "matter" and "antimatter" for survival and growth are "self-fulfilled" through the supporting structure of mother, father and other family members. When the baby grows up she/he comes in touch with more matter goods in family, school and external environment, a sense of addiction develops unlimitedly which not only result in unhappiness but produce many complex problems including attitude of violence; affecting adversely the intellect-emotion-spirit with a skewed consciousness. Problems like crimes of passion, distorted relationship, virtual pleasure, mad-race for money at the cost of all other determinants of happy life etc emerge.

A child grows in a society, which is changing since evolution of mankind. Depending on the social order humans are molded influencing their behavior and interface with various social forces prevalent at a particular point of time. It is said that we now have six times purchasing power than our parents. In spite of higher economic power, there is decline in degree of happiness. Life has become more transient in the present era of globalization with increasing violence in different and new forms, which is stratifying the human family instead of consolidating it as one world one human family. It has further created few islands of prosperity amidst large mass of poverty. The prosperity is not accompanied by peace as result violence like terrorism is spreading its roots throughout the world at a faster rate. In such a global social order individual rights and liberties are subjected to coercive state instead of providing security for persons and their properties. Justice, equality, empathy and conflict, dispute resolution mechanism etc are not able to operate in time as a result there is chaos in the society instead of order. The disintegration of social order is further accentuated by mostly negative values and norms that the individuals somehow have managed to internalize. With such disorderliness in society, happiness remains a distant dream, in spite of increased mobility, connectivity, and high technology and prosperity. Such a state of affair in today's globalization era may lead to "fundamentalist individualism" destroying the societal functions, like mutual dependency, visibility, extensiveness, groups and networks, honor, values and norms and the most vital "the order". The human will be transformed to a money-earning robot, which will have no subtle or causal body. All the roots of spirit and emotion will be redundant.

Sometime back, a team of researchers in Europe have deliberated on happiness and cost of producing it in terms of money. They have questioned 10,000 people in Europe to find out effects of money and life style on emotion including happiness and satisfaction. In particular, the respondents were asked things which give them happiness. The feedback of respondents were weighed in a Life-satisfaction scale of one (almost suicidal) to seven (euphoric). With these data, they calculated how far changes in life style and social relationships would move the average person up in the scale and then put a "price" on social and life style factors. The reality has emerged- that is the money people earned made a relatively minor contribution to the level of personal happiness. The researchers also concluded that materialistic values are counter-productive over time; rather they heighten insecurity, a main cause of unhappiness.

The research findings highlight that the life style issues to acquire happiness are-

1) Fit and healthy bodies-excellent health was the equivalent of roughly US$ 600,000.0 per year.
2) Meeting friends frequently worth US$12, 5000.0
3) Living with some one-worth US$10, 5000.0
4) Married life worth US$10, 5000.0
5) Chatting regularly with neighbors worth US$800,000.0

Thus the researchers infer that the importance of income and exercise of power have very little to do with happiness in life. Such result of the research was expected. It is not something new. In AD 785 **Abd Er-Rahman** emir of Co'rdoba wrote the following lines towards end of his life- "I have now reigned 50 years.... beloved by my subjects, dreaded by my enemies and respected by my allies. Riches and honors, power and pleasure have waited on my call, nor does any earthly blessing appear to have wanted my felicity. In this situation, I have diligently numbered the days of pure and genuine happiness which have fallen to my lot. They amount to fourteen".

Happiness and Peace for Social Order

13
Peace

PEACE AND HUNGER

All the expectations of "Globalization "have gone wrong within 2-3 decades of its beginning. The statement of Executive Director, World Bank Juan kosh Dabob while addressing a conference at Singapore University on May 20,2008 is revealing, which highlight that the recent global food price increase during last few years has produced globally 100 million poor people Since 2002, food price has increased two and half times mainly because of decreased investment level in agriculture, increase in oil price, increased demand for food, trade barriers and climate change etc. Is Globalization heading for untimely death?

Globalization tall claims have become valueless, when the humanity has failed to remove hunger with all kinds of technological innovations sugar coating the human minds with glamorous outbursts of extremely few affluent people; which have pushed back the real problems of humanity to a corner and blocked the channels of "thought energy" to innovate ideas and solutions for problems like hunger and violence.

Basically, humanity has to realize that "hunger leads to violence ". Because hunger is uneasy or painful sensation caused by want of food/nutrients essential for survival. It is a desire not for sake of desire but a dire necessity to sustain life. The world hunger today is caused by the aggregated scarcity of food at the level of the world as a whole. Malnutrition, a word used for lack of required nutrition to maintain a healthy body and mind. It leads to state of hunger. Protein energy malnutrition (PEM) is the a very lethal form of malnutrition/hunger, which is lack of calories and protein. The recent estimate of FAO indicates that 854 million people globally are undernourished, constituting 12.60% of present 7.0 billion population of the world. Out of 854 million, 820 million are in developing countries. Second type of malnutrition/hunger is the lack of micro nutrients. It is vitamins and minerals. In developing countries 1 out of 3 people are deficient in micronutrients according to WHO. Between 100 to 140 million children are Vitamin A-deficient. It is estimated that 250,000 to 500,000 vitamin A-deficient children become blind every year, half of them dying within 12 months of losing sight. Similarly Iron deficiency causes anemia which impairs physical and cognitive development. Two billion people (about 30% of world's population) are anemic.20% of maternal deaths of pregnant women is from iron deficiency. Under micronutrients Iodine deficiency disorders affect children's mental health. As per WHO 50.0 million people have some degree of mental problems because of Iodine deficiency. All these deficiencies constitute hunger.

Mankind is always on a continuous basis concern for hunger which gives rise to other problems like violence and socio-economic disorder. The UN organized first world Food conference at Rome in 1974, which highlighted the following-

(a) Hundreds of Millions of world people are undernourished. Population growth is adding 75 to 80 million more people each year, 200,000 each day. Within the next 25 years or so the present numbers of 4 billion will be nearly 7 billion. They all must be fed.

(b) Stocks of grain have hit all-time low since the end of World War II Surplus stocks formerly held in reserve have nearly been exhausted and no longer offer security against widespread hunger and starvation.

(c) Less of cheaper protein foods, which normally supplement grain diets is available. The world's fish catch and per capita production of protein-rich legumes, the staple diet in many countries have declined.

(d) Food shortages have created unrest in many parts of the world, are particularly severe in countries where hunger and the diseases that thrive on under-nourished bodies are prevalent. This scarcity has been aggravated by the consumption of more and more grain to produce meat, egg and milk.

(e) Mounting fertilizers and energy shortages are reducing food production in certain areas and increasing food prices.

From 1974 to 2008, the world hunger crisis has aggravated manifold in spite of technological advancement. The UN Food Agriculture Organization estimated in 2006 that

854 million people world wise is undernourished, which is 12.60% of world population. Hunger facts also highlight that the children are most viable victims of hunger. Poorly nourished children suffer up to 160 days of illness each year, at least half of 10.90 million child death takes place each year. The undernourished is also a cause for death- 61% diarrhea, 61% malaria, 57% pneumonia and 56% measles.

In developing countries, malnutrition, as measured by studying affects 32% of children- one of three in 200. Geographically more than 70% of malnourished children live in Asia,26% in Africa and 4% in Latin America and Caribbean.

These are only some of the statistics on world hunger. The real life figures could be so threatening that one would be scared to think about it. It is obvious because today's humanity fall short of required IQ, EQ &SQ to meet the challenge of world hunger. With only IQ and without EQ and SQ it will be impossible to solve the problem of hunger.

It is also admitted that poverty is the principal cause of hunger.2004 statistics of the World Bank came out in 2008 have estimated that there were an estimated 982 million people in the developing countries who live on $1.0 a day or less. Progress in poverty reduction has been concentrated in Asia, especially East Asia with major improvement taking place in China. In sub-Saharan Africa, the number of people in extreme poverty has increased.

Let us realize that hunger is also a cause of poverty, by causing poor health, low level of energy intake leading to people's inability to work and earn and worst impact is mental impairment like negative behavioral traits, jealousy, anger and last but not the least is violent responses ending up with life style of criminals, terrorists etc. Today the humanity is so engrossed with so called technological advancement which is destructive for majority and constructive for few. We have forgotten that a hunger free world will get rid of violence, crime and terror etc and result in a culture of Peace. To work towards this basic, one single human failure to control and limit increasing number of human species is threatening the history of humanity. Overpopulation touches every aspect of our planet's life. We have only one planet, the Earth which supports life. It is gifted with life-support systems and resources to feed the humanity. But there is a limit to this. How long and to what extent it can feed without destroying itself? Feeding the humanity is not an isolated phenomenon. It is linked to all activities of humans like economy, social, environmental, technological, spatial (human settlements), military and all other activities and relationships between the humans and the planet earth. While analyzing capacity of the planet to feed us, it is observed that more of us are eating more and better than ever before. Cereal consumption of the world has doubled since 1970 and meat production has tripled since 1961. Global fish catch grew more than six times from 1950 to 1977. But to what extent the world can increase its harvest at this rate? Can it feed extra 75 million people born annually? The silver lining is with the global population doubled to 6 billion in 40 years from 1960, although the global food production kept up figure wise basing on required per capita consumption, but access to food grew unevenly. Haves and have-nots are at loggerhead as overpopulation exploited the resources of the planet beyond its regenerative capacity. After utilizing the world's best cropland, the farmers are utilizing increasingly marginal land. The fertility of good crop land is on decline due to top soil loss and soil degradation. This has resulted in reduced global productivity by 13% in last fifty years. Pesticides losing their effectiveness as the pests acquire more resistance. Water, key to crop production is progressively unavailable for agriculture. Biotechnology in principle may produce drought-resistant varieties that withstand pest attack and new high yielding crops. But strong debate globally is on for and against for GMF. Fear is growing for erosion of genetic resources in thousands of traditional varieties grown across the world No one knows definitely if all such interventions with the resources of earth are resulting in climate change or climate change has adverse impact on food production.

Another disturbing factor is that humans are trying to acquire food security endangering food needs of other life forms in the earth who contribute substantially to keep the planet alive. This is quite evident from-

(a) Amount of nitrogen available for uptake by plants is much higher than the natural level and has more than doubled since 1940s.

(b) The excess nitrogen comes from fertilizers running off farmland, from live stock manure and from other human activities.

(c) It is changing the composition of species in ecosystems, reducing soil fertility, depleting ozone layer and intensifying climate change etc.

(d) Globally 26% of the earth's land area, nearly 3.3 billion hectares has been taken over for crop land and pasture replacing a third of temperate and tropical forests and a quarter of natural grass land to feed increasing human population.

(e) 0.50 billion hectares has been converted to urban and built up areas.

Human habitats destroying natural ecosystems resulting in extinction of many other species Some of critical facts stated above which affect the normal functioning of planet earth is gradually reducing its productive capacity to feed the increasing number of humans. It is to be realized that basically planet earth or a life form including human is an entity of energy. Free flow of energy in the planet earth is now getting blocked due to extreme intervention of human activities giving rise to loss of equilibrium between natural(solar energy power system),domesticated(subsidized solar power system) and fabricated(fuel-powered system). This is a serious problem of destroying the planet; as a result hunger crisis may accelerate. As is evident now, with all kinds of technology and empty slogans of globalization and MDGs, in 2003, 842 million people did not have enough to eat according to UN's Food and Agriculture Organization. Hunger and malnutrition killed 10 million people a year globally-25000 a day-one life extinguished every five seconds. It can be assumed that world does produce till now enough to feed every one today. But food is in the wrong place or unaffordable or cannot be stored long enough. So making sure everyone has enough to eat is more about politics than science. Politicians give different statements at different times. The war of words - how long the politicians will continue with such gimmicks? It is most desirable that "war of words" is replaced by "peace of words" to ensure that relationship between countries, cultures, religions, and individuals are not strained and problems are settled amicably and peacefully what the intellectuals say? University of Arizona, USA conducted a study on food security in USA. The highlights are as follows-

(a) Save Earth-Cutting food waste will go a long way towards reducing serious environmental problems Reducing food waste by half can reduce the adverse environmental impact by 25%.

(b) Throw-Away Society-America has long been poster child for the "throw-away" society. As much as 40-50% of all food ready for harvest never gets eaten.

(c) Never Opened-On average, households in America waste 14% of food purchases. A family discards 1.28 pounds of food a day, about 470 pounds a household a year.15% of that includes products still within their expiration date but never opened.

(d) Billions Binned- Household food waste alone adds up to $43.0 billion. Americas threw out about three times as much food in 2004 as they did 20 years back. 30% of milk and other dairy products grain products, fresh fruits and vegetables were tossed while 15% of meat, dried beans, nuts and processed fruits and vegetables were disposed in landfills.

It is also known that-

(a) 5% of America's leftovers can feed 4 million people for a day.
(b) Disposing of food waste costs the US $ 1.0 billion a year.

Rotting food releases methane- a more potent greenhouse gas than carbon dioxide which today in the days of political supremacy listens to intellectual's voice? Politicians and Political institutions are becoming more egoistic day by day developing a motive of self-benefit and benefit for dear and near ones than the millions of hungry people. More slogans, talks, negotiations at global, international and national and local level continue at the cost of huger crisis. Political or any ego gives rise to hidden anger and intolerance leading to a violent psychic. In the name of some plea or other the leaders think and act irrationally in a self-centered manner, the responses of which spread violence and terror as quite a large number of people starve aggravating hunger crisis converting them to fundamentalist which they express through increasing crime and terror. Religion which is misinterpreted adds up to the violent psychic. Peace is ignored as a powerful tool and technology which has the capacity of solving all kinds of problems emerging from human relationships and their intervention with the earth's resources. Failure to conceive and act on this concept in

the evolution process will change the genetical make-up of humans and simultaneously blocking the free energy flow in the seven energy centers of humans as a result they cannot think and act rationally. Perhaps, this was one of the reasons; the humans almost became extinct in 70,000 B.C. according to a study of American Journal of Human Genetics. The study highlights that number of humans may have shrunk to as low as 2000 before it began to rise again in the Stone Age. It is a lesson of the history to be learnt from the behavior of humans 20,000 years back-extremes of humans led to climate and hunger crisis which reduced human population to edge of extinction.

After looking at the past and also the present, let us concentrate and apply IQ, EQ, and SQ to meet the challenges of world hunger which is linked to earth's health and its resources. It is high time for the humanity to realize that the root cause of hunger is both Biosphere and human violence As such we have to develop conviction that the world hunger crisis can only be solved sustainly with adoption of "inclusive and holistic" faculty which is only the Peace and its technologies It may sound utopian as constituents of Peace are still beyond our perception. The crude materialism followed today is anti-peace in nature, which will kill the essence of human values and rights. With Peace as the technology, we will be able to develop harmonious human relations and humanitarian values enabling us to overcome world food crisis, terror, deaths and destruction.

What are the constituents of Peace? How Peace is made up? What are its technologies? All these questions are to be answered. Peace is extremely high frequency energy. It has a hierarchical pyramidal structure- the apex of which is Absolute Energy of Consciousness - the supreme energy which controls everything in the universe. It is the WILL of supreme energy that decides all activities taking place in the universe. It is not known how the WILL of Supreme Energy decides, operates and functions. In the pyramid of energy, next to Supreme Energy is cosmic, spiritual consciousness and matter energy which interact and support all structures of the universe. Cosmic energy which stimulates spiritual and consciousness energy activates energy entities for functioning of the biotic and abiotic components of the earth, besides other activities of the universe. The "matter energy" is predominantly in the hands of the homo sapiens- a complex species that channelize the energy both for constructive and destructive purposes. When the use of this energy is not in conformity with the law of universal energy, the process of destruction in the earth is accelerated creating serious problems in the functioning of earth and human activities. Today, the humans are at this cross-road of evolution.

There are billions of channels for peace energy to flow. Any blockage of flow of peace energy in the channels disturbs the equilibrium and give rise to violence. Peace energy is always positive mainly consisting of truth, order and harmony of universal power house. Technologies are to be innovated to utilize peace energy to solve various problems confronted by the humanity including the crisis of hunger. This calls for convergence of IQ, EQ and SQ through natural philosophical process of "collective minds" and eternity of truth, order and harmony networking with biosphereism and humanitarianism. This will determine the preferential order as security (personal, food, shelter, socio-economic, livelihood, environmental and all other kinds of security that establishes equilibrium between biotic and abiotic components of the universe), comfort with a sense of enoughness and happiness.

Quantum Physics tells us that we live in a world of energy. It has also discovered that matter is not matter but it is energy. Energy creates things and also modifies when required. Higher form of energy is Peace energy which actually creates, manages, and recreates bio-energy. If the earth energy channel is blocked, free flow of energy is interrupted as a result production of goods like food for survival diminishes and hunger strikes the world. Another cause of hunger can be attributed to over population and excessive violent intervention of humans in the earth energy.

This results in global hunger, violence especially terrorism declining the values of biosphereism and humanitarianism and products and events in the earth and the universe. Both earth energy and cosmic energy, collectively create life-force energy. The earth force energy creates products like food, minerals, and other life-support products for survival of humans and other life forms, which are termed as bio-energy. If the earth energy channel is blackened, free flow of energy is interrupted as a result production of goods like food for survival diminishes and hunger strikes the world. Another cause of hunger can be attributed to over population and excessive violent intervention of humans in the earth energy. This results in global hunger, violence especially terrorism declining the values of biosphereism and humanitarianism.

With this perception of Peace and its technology, I place below some of my view point's which need to be weaved into a gigantic web converging with other ideas in order to overcome the world hunger crisis and create wealth and prosperity distributed evenly to all world citizens The first and foremost principle of Peace and its technology is the adoption of "Policies of inclusiveness and holisticness". To overcome hunger crisis, all other aspects of human activities are to be based on the basic principle of "inclusiveness", which means everyone in the earth is exposed to the problems equally and every one also shares the benefits equally.

Food security, Energy security, life security, socio-economic security and political security etc should be collectively tackled through Peace process identifying billions of channels of connectivity between humans and eco-resources to ensure free flow of Peace energy. Optimum size of human population in the planet earth should be proactively decided considering available resources of the planet and their regenerative and recycling capacity in addition to adoption of new family planning techniques like Norplant (product of Finland), a contraceptive capsule implanted in the skin delivers a constant hormonal dose for a period of five years etc. While adopting policies to tackle over population it must also simultaneously be ensured that rights of children born are provided with appropriate security starting from food, energy to socio-economic and environmental so that they develop a sense of enoughness to meet their basic needs for contributing to a safer world to live in.

Earth energy use must ensure that the elements of life-support systems like land, water, air, energy, climate, biodiversity etc are conserved simultaneously increasing the production and productive from these resources to meet the human needs. For example a "new green revolution" can be started with use of bio-fertilizer like Vermiculture, biomass and bio-pesticides etc and totally discarding use of chemical fertilizer. This will enable most of the dead soil now to regain life through which sustainable level of production can be achieved. Food and Energy security are interlinked. Today there is over dependence on oil energy throughout the world. This has resulted in high increase in oil price. In May 2008 per barrel price of oil has gone up to $ 135.0 which is almost double of the price which was there before six months. The food price rise globally is continuing now because of this increase in oil price. Oil producing countries have perhaps reduced their production to fetch high income for their countries. When the demand increases, production is less as a result the price is skyrocketed. This is one of the basic reasons of high food price and hunger. If this conspiracy of artificial oil crisis succeeds, there will be serious crisis of hunger globally resulting in a catastrophe after which there will be no one left to tell the tale of humanity. This is to be seriously considered and oil producing countries should be urged upon to be humanitarian in their approach adopting the principle "we have to learn to let live" and increase the quantity of production of oil to stabilize its price not only to reduce hunger but also for other activities. Another source of energy much talked about is Nuclear energy which is infinite. But there is danger of using it for production of Nuclear weapons. Unless there is truthful global understanding and agreement not to use it for production of Nuclear weapons, this energy can be put to use for power production which can solve many energy problems. Its harmful effects should be totally eliminated and appropriate technology should be developed for disposal of its waste without any adverse effect on environment. However the future most sustainable and peace and eco-friendly source of energy is solar-Hydrogen based, for which there is urgent need take up research to design cost-effective technology. With this energy when available will be able to solve the hunger crisis besides making all other human activities peaceful and sustainable. Presently oil price is declining. We have to watch and see how the price of food and other materials will be influenced.

Hunger is also linked to psychic of humans. The big question is-"We eat to live" or "we live to eat". If we eat to live, then to a great extent hunger problem will be solved. Because we understand the essence of life by ensuring that we support others besides ourselves to meet the hunger problem for all people living in any part of the world. This will promote a healthy and peaceful life for all. When we eat to live, holistic intelligence is developed to a living environment for all, which will be socially satisfying, economically viable and peaceful. A sense of enoughness is developed to consume resources so that others have also equal access to resources to live in a hunger free world. But unfortunately, today we are addicted to the psychic of "We live to eat", as if we live for eternity and consume all resources without sharing with others. We do not realize the painful hunger crisis of other members of our human family. This has resulted in loss of human values and twisted our life styles to acquire more and more assets not necessary for a peaceful living. Rather such people live a miserable life and die also miserably. The entire gamut of employment/livelihood program is structured accordingly resulting in unemployment of large number of people leading them to live in hunger. When discrimination is created in employment program, we indulge in high profile deliberations of poverty reduction which fails in real life situation. This gives rise to death, destruction and produces a large human force that become violent and ultimately transformed themselves to the status of terrorists. As such we must adopt the principles of "we eat to live" to create a hunger free world. With a hunger free world, violence like war, crime and terrorism etc can be eliminated and replaced by peace energy to cope with problems like hunger, high food price and instability of other socio-economic determinants. This will lead the humanity in the path of "prosperity through peace" which will not only solve the world hunger crisis but reestablish social and family ethics eliminating psychological disturbances like drugs, alcohol addiction, teen age pregnancy and divorce etc. It is suggested that peace education should be made mandatory from "womb to tomb" which will be a continuous learning lesson to heal, purify and unify the humanity with application of cosmic and earth energy principles. A perception needs to be developed that "if he lives hunger free and peacefully, I live hunger free and peacefully". We must all collectively work together as one human family imprinting in our minds "Peace" as the basic life-support system and discard all kinds of violence and terror to overcome the world hunger crisis.

In developing countries the crisis of hunger is more severe. The land use of such countries has not been properly planned and utilized to bring equilibrium between land required for production of food to overcome hunger and for other needs like industry, habitats and other needs. The technology for production of food has not yet percolated to zero ground level to increase both production and productivity. In many countries the virtual glamour of cities pulling the farmers from field with expectation of acquiring more wealth, but they become burden on cities instead of assets. In some countries highly subsidized food make people idle and they expect more from governments as a result hunger crisis acclerates. People must work in the field to yield more food and governments should provide requiired inputs and support so that they are not pushed out towards cities. If this happens, there will be serious conflict between fabricated and domesticated landscape. Food production must be developed as a sophisticated profession and provided with high quality of socio-economic infrastructure, amenities and facilities to improve the quality of life of people, which can be compareable to quality of life of people living in good cities to make them happy and provide them with peace for a sustainable and prosperous living. They should also enjoy a status in the society. Holistic approach must be adopted to food production so that the crisis of hunger can be overcome. Food security and freedom from hunger should be linked with all other kinds of social, economic and environmental security to develop cofidence of food production workers so that on a sustainable basis food is available to all, keeping in view the rate of growth of population.

> A hungry man
> Is helpless and dies silently
> An affluent man
> Throws away his food
> As waste
> And never cares for the
> Man dying hungry
> A paradox
> Needs to be realized
> To replace violent outburst
> With energy of Peace
> To develop a culture
> Where no man dies
> Of Hunger.

14
Peace

PEACE & VIOLENCE

What went wrong with Cho Seung-Hui, a 23 years student at Virginia Tech University on 16 April 2007? Cho, from South Korea was living in USA since 1992 with his family in centreville, Virginia. At 7.15 am local time on 16 April 2007, Cho entered west Ambier Johnston Hall, a dormitory housing where some 900 students were staying and shot down two students. Cho and the entire Virginia Tech University remained calm after the shooting killing two students. Then after about 2 hours at about past 9.0 am, Cho rushed into Norris Hall in Room-207 with two handguns and shot German instructor Christopher James Bishop in the head. Then he shot a girl in her mouth, a boy in the legs and shot after shot he killed 32 people of the university and finally killed himself.

This was not the first incident in a highly prosperous country like USA. Violent act perpetrated by and on youth, although received wide media as well as political attention, no political leader stood up to debate on gun-drug-violence control issues.

In general overall problem of violence among youth is consistent with socio cultural context generating violent impulses entering the minds of the youths. The impulses are quickly processed in their minds, creating violent outburst. The university of Illinois, Chicago and university of Wisconsin, Milwaukee jointly identified the model of basic clusters of functional outcomes produce by violent or potentially violent episodes, which is placed below.

However violence is not only a simple response to socio cultural factors. Biological, environmental and behavioral factors also determine violent/non-violent attitude/ response. The level of hormones and neurotransmitters are significant part of biological effects. Testosterone has effects on the probability of aggressive responses to environmental events. Androgens appeared to be altering the response to aggression-provoking stimuli. Levels of certain neurotransmitters in critical regions of the brain result from accumulated life experiences forming the substrata of behavior. The effects of operation of three basic neurotransmitters namely dopamine, serotonin and norepinephrine, Embry and Flannery state are to great extent are well established.

Rewards, social recognition release dopamine in the nucleus accumbens and ventral tegnmental areas, which communicate with regions in the mesocortex, cortex and frontal lobes forming the basis for long term planning. Touch, affection and positive status release serotonin which inhibits aggressive behavior by stimulating serotonergic axons in the forebrain and amygdala. Low level of serotonin gives rise to depression and aggressive behavior, whereas high level of serotonin associated with non-violent behavior. Adequate level of dopamine improves positive behavioral control and social responsiveness. The level of dopamine increases with social and affectionate stimuli like kind words praise and physical touch. It is well established that levels of serotonin increase in both the recipient and the giver in these exchanges.

Threat, coercion and negative environmental impulses decrease available serotonin and release norepiniphine, cortisol and other hormones and neurotransmitters which increase aggression and violence. Thus it can be surmised that biological factors also affect the probability that violent action will occur by changing sensitivity to the environmental events. Anti-social and violent youths are the product of combination of factors like chaotic and coercive parenting, poverty and side by side path way crisis of overdose of affluence, drug abuse, family violence, different forms of harsh inconsistent behavior, company of anti-social children/friends in school, colleges and work places, exposure to media glorifying sex and violence, lack of access to food, job and shelter security, and coercive processes to justice system, education and social relations etc. Citizen's indifference attitude to absence of political will to curb drug-gun-violence culture also contributes from individual violent behavior to societal and national violence. Cho, the 23 years youth of Virginia has fallen victim to some of the above biological, socio-cultural and environmental systems of one of the most prosperous countries of the world, the USA. Is it not a warning bell for the entire humanity? And what is going to be the response to such anti-social and violent power with a wide range of undesirable side effects?

The response should evolve violence prevention programmes through Peace Building menu, with the younger children even from the child in the mother's womb. Biologically, can the scientific community advance knowledge from "Stem Cell" research and induce unspecialized cells in the brain which will release adequate quantity of serotonin and dopamine to generate violent –free and peaceful responses? The "Stem Cell" research should be conducted in this direction, so that biologically human species become peaceful. Besides, principles of socio-cultural learning emphasizing peace power modules should be embedded in the cultural entities – family, schools, organizations, agencies and work places, and communities etc.

The role of the society / nations should not be only limited to constructing factories for producing money / material prosperity, but it shall have the bounden duty to transform the society/ nation to an entity of "Wholeness of Peace" by eliminating generation of conflict/violent impulses/responses and through improving the situations at the personal, relational, structural and cultural level.

Recognizing and analyzing the destructive power of visible (direct violence) and invisible(cultural and structural violence), principles of designing of education system and social learning process should be reoriented and promoted with reinforcing actions by parents, teachers, staff and other community members as well as youth themselves. Political organizations should be revamped and irrespective party lines, politics as a structured system should unanimously design and implement policies to counter both visible and invisible violence by adopting "Peace" as a critical input to all kinds of human activities and development programmes.

If the humanity adopts this broad approach to Peace Building Process, human species like Cho will in course of time disappear completely from the society. High level of research should be initiated in the sector by establishing institutions like National Peace Academy in each and every country of the world, who shall be given the responsibility to design conflict transformation service and Peace Building Process by networking the organs of the society like family, schools, colleges, universities, work organizations and communities etc to solve the most challenging problem of violence – the world is facing today. There should be a time bound programme, failing which culture of violence will overtake the humanity and wipe out its existence from the biosphere.

15
Peace

PEACE ENERGY AND ANTIMATTER

The ideas with recent scientific discovery researched for last 60 years creating molecules of positronium – a short lived atom that comprises both matter and antimatter. This discovery helps not only the development of "fusion power" of "positivity" but also spur explanation for a long standing enigma about universe. Besides, negatively it can also be used for directed – energy weapons such as gamma-ray lasers.

Matter is well understood. I add one new dimension to matter – it has built in it both violent and peace energy in various proportions. It has more violent energy than peace energy. With this new dimension of matter, I place before the world citizens the logical hypothesis of Antimatter and its crucial role in generating peace energy.

Antimatter is made up of particles smaller than what might be called an "anti-atom". These particles are equal and opposite of their matter counterparts. It is the "mirror" of matter. It is equal yet opposite, a pair of identical twins with opposite personalities. A positron, the anti-electron has a positive charge and opposite spin. An anti-proton has a negative charge and the opposite spin of its matter counterpart. Anti-neutrons only have opposite spin but both are neutral charge.

Thus antimatter is a partner of matter and in principle that could be another world from these partner particles. But in reality, both the partners Matter and Antimatter created the universe by coming together. Like matter, in antimatter also I add a new dimension – it consists more peace energy and less violent energy which is just opposite of matter.

The Big Bang theory of creation universe tells us that the universe began from a "singularity" – a tiny point. This tiny point scientifically, I deduced as existence of "matter" and "antimatter" side by side for a long time before the collision between the two took place. Some scientists believe that there was no "time" before the Big Bang, which according to me is not correct. The "Singularity" was existing for a long time and at a particular "time" the matter and antimatter of this tiny particles collided, which was for a very brief "time" again and annihilated each other in flash of energy as a result both the matter and antimatter no longer existed and a proportionally large amount of energy – the Absolute energy of consciousness / Universal peace conscious energy is released. This can be termed also as Absolute creative energy, as the Antimatter with high level of peace energy conquered the violent energy of matter to produce creative construction-the universe. Only peace energy is creative whereas the violent energy is destructive. The Absoluteness of energy generated comprises broadly of five kinds namely cosmic, spiritual, consciousness, conscious and matter energy. These five sources of energy are capable of constructing various types of matters and forces. Immediately after annihilation the Absolute in form of a fireball emerged and expanded and it began to cool and produced tiny particles of energy and matter, each of them much smaller than atoms forming a thick soup-like materials. After about three minutes of annihilation, gravity started to pull the particles and joint together to form gases such as hydrogen and helium. By the end of three minutes the matter that surrounds us today has been created.

Over time, as the young universe grew larger, gases clumped into clouds. After several millions years the cloud began to form stars, galaxies and the solar systems including our planet earth where only life germinated with creation of life support system such as air, water and fire/energy.

In course of evolution process, the most intelligent life species, the Homo dominated and manipulated biosphere and planet earth with single minded objective of generating prosperity only for themselves at the cost of all others. In this process they discover more and more use of matter energy like chemical energy, electrical energy, potential energy, nuclear energy, kinetic energy, sound energy, heat energy, light energy and electromagnetic energy etc. Unhealthy the competitions and conflicts grew within the homo species creating more and more destructive weapons through use of matter and its energy. As a result, there is now more creative destruction. Time is ripe now to reverse the process to create more peaceful creative construction failing which the humans will be wiped out from the earth. In order to fulfill this objective the use of matter and antimatter should be explored in a way to ensure that the principles of antimatter where peace energy is at high level compared to matter is put into practice establishing connectivity of matter energy with other four kinds of energy and incorporating the concept of Absolute energy of consciousness to create peaceful products and services, to be at peace at each and every individual level and ultimately contributing to peace of humans, the earth and the universe as a whole. The antimatter has to be fully explored to generate more and more peace energy so that when it collides with matter, peace energy will dominate and apply to matter and antimatter for production of peaceful and sustainable goods and services to prolong the life of the universe as a peaceful entity. This calls for retuning of human thought and emotion so that appropriate activities are designed to achieve the event of "Ultimate reality" of life – The Peace.

Throughout the human civilization, many people had thought and deliberated on peace. At random, I have selected two names from 19th-20th century. They are Alfred Nobel, Albert Einstein. During their lifetimes, they became different from the mainstream of violent human society and contributed intellectually and financially to promote peace culture in the world.

Alfred Nobel (October 21, 1833 – December 10, 1896) was a chemist, engineer, innovator, armaments manufacturer, inventor of dynamite and extended financial support for promotion of world peace generation after generation which still continue and will continue indefinitely, unless the world is annihilated by the increasing violent forces generated day by day. Alfred Nobel, a descended of the seventeenth century scientist Olaus Rudbeck (1630-1708) was the third son of Immanuel Nobel (1801-1872) and Andriette Ahlsell Nobel (1805-1889). His father invented modern plywood and then started a torpedo work. Alfred studied chemistry. Due to bankruptcy of his family business, Alfred devoted to study of explosive and use of nitroglycerin. He invented dynamite and Gelignite or blasting gelatin which was more powerful than dynamite. Many countries of the world opened such explosive factories and Alfred as the inventor received substantial share of the proceed from each factory making him that time one of the wealthiest man in the world.

His explosive factories had killed many people including his younger brother Emil. The then society called Alfred as a "the merchant of death". Such events in his life brought about changes in his decision to leave a better legacy after his death. Keeping this thought process in mind he laid the foundation of Nobel Prize in 1895, which he wrote in his will. He left behind 31 million kronor (4,223,500 USD in 1896 which in 2007 it is 103,931,888 USD. Since 1901 prizes were awarded for eminence in physical science, chemistry and medical science and the fourth is called for literary work.

Alfred Nobel was unmarried. In 1876 Bertha von Suttner became Albert's secretary, but only after brief stay she left and married Baron Arthur. In spite of her marriage, she maintained personal contact with Alfred through correspondence with him until her death in 1896. During these 20 years she was the major influence and motivated Alfred to include a Peace prize recognizing peace as "ultimate reality" of life.

Alfred was convinced about relevance of peace power to save the humans in comparison to his explosive power which killed many humans. As a result Nobel Peace Prize was installed and Bertha von Suttner, the lady who infused the power of peace in Alfred's mind was awarded with the first Nobel Peace Prize in 1905. Alfred before his death has changed from creator of destructive energy with explosive power to a creator of constructive energy through peace power. Today he symbolizes Peace and a person rendering the greatest service to the cause of international fraternity life which is full of ups and downs.

Albert Einstein- His curiosity in science developed when he was 4 to5 years old watching invariable northward swing of the needle in a magnetic compass. But his life and career was not smooth. He was very independent minded and did not obey the arbitrary orders giving by the school Authority. He was expelled from the school after which he moves to Munich to finish his schooling. He renounced the German citizenship in 1896 and subsequently he was granted Swiss citizenship in 1901. He graduated from Aarau in 1900 as a teacher of mathematics and physics. With hurdles in path of life he continuously went up and up in the ladder of his life and was ultimately awarded with Nobel Prize in 1921. Reaching at the highest intellectual level, he gave two historic statements quoted below: "We scientist, whose drastic destiny it has been to help make the methods of annihilation ever more gruesome and more effective, must consider it our solemn and transcendent duty to do all in our power in preventing these weapons being used.......... What task could possibly be more important to us?" Human being a part of a whole called universe, a part limited to time and space, experiences himself his thoughts and feelings had something separated from the rest – a kind of optical delusion of "consciousness". This delusion is a kind of prison for us restricting us to our personal desires and to affection for few persons nearest us. Our task must be to free from ourselves from the prison by widening our circle of compassion to embrace all living creatures and the whole of Nature of beauty".

Thus Einstein has gone down in the history of human civilization as a "Great Man" of Peace than a scientist through his insistence and persistence at trying to achieve a global peace, nuclear disarmament have brought us far along in rebuilding a global society since the second world war". Albert Einstein was a positive force contributing to the knowledge and humanitarianism of the world through Peace as the instrument. Einstein equation of energy needs to be expanded as he himself said that human is a fraction of universe and his matter energy equation can only work within the framework of "Consciousness"

Peace Energy and AntiMatter

16
Peace

CONFLICTS & TERRORISM

Some of the ideas which can minimize conflicts in community are-

1) Concern for others and honor every person's ideas and skills.
2) Interact with your conscience to resolve conflicts in a peaceful manner.
3) Adopt TRUTH, ORDER AND HARMONY as the guiding principles of your life.
4) Equity in sharing of community's resources.
5) Reinforce the family with love, affection, care and share attitude, feeling for each other, discarding negative feelings, ego, hatred, jealousy etc.
6) Be open to alternative options to community problems.
7) Understanding, adjustment and tolerance to perceive conflicts so that everyone will be as open as possible to transform conflicts into peace.
8) Community members should be supportive towards each other rather than judgmental.
9) Adopt proactive attitude to avoid conflict.
10) Social responsibility and continuous learning process to be put into practice through capacity building of community members.

Once inner and external conflicts are transformed to value based concepts and actions, we will be able to create propane community, where crimes, violence, terrorism etc will vanish from the world.

I have highlighted some ideas to free our planet from terrorism through Mind Bending process. This time I share some ideas to free our planet from terrorism through Mind Mending approach. Mind Mending is a long term process to completely erase terrorism from the earth. This process attempts to reduce the responses of reptile mind and to increase the role of mammalian cortex parts of the brain. Although this is a long drawn process, scientific, philosophical, psychological and environmental measures are to be designed and given highest priority for their application to change the genetical make-up of humans. His neuroanatomical structure is strengthened for self- enlightenment instead of self- destruction for killing others as invisible enemy. This process has to begin from the stage of formation of neural plate in the mother's womb through imprinting appropriate impulses from like tender loving care, affection, concern for others etc through romantic husband-wife relation, increasing body pleasure level, happy family and community environment, caring and sharing attitude for others etc. Peace education should be started from mother's womb and continues till one goes to grave. It should be taught from nursery level to highest level of education. In organizations/institutions, the working environment should be designed with peace as the foundation with the components of security, comfort with a sense of enoughness and pleasure linked to antimatter components like Truth, Order and

Harmony. This implies that in all stages of life "science of spirituality" should be converged with "science of Matter". Matter in no case is allowed to over ride the mind. If this happens, there will be more "creative destruction" than "creative construction". The mind should be always be tuned for positive thoughts to improve neurochemistry and neurology of behavior. The impulses from family, community, society, economic and political organizations should be peaceful in order to make the responses of humans peaceful." Collectiveness" welfare should replace "self welfare".

Such Mind Mending approach will create propane individual and community so that the word "terrorism" is erased from the minds of humans.

Are we capable of doing this? If we develop determination it can be easily done. Our incapability of doing this will take us quickly to the "doomsday".

Think about it and spread this message to free our planet from terrorism.

Terrorism is a present form of violence aims at mass killing by the 'invisible' enemy. The humans who are products of Nature and members of one species are killing each others as each member is not able to meet his basic needs and tries to snatch away other's resources which are more than his needs; and it serves only his greasing the process of Terrorism. People involved come up with all sorts of pleas like religious, dominance of one group on others, neglect to fulfill the basic needs of all people of the planet earth etc, by giving hollow slogans.

The basic problem with human intellect is that we are incapable of nipping the problem at the bud. We watch and see and continue discussions, during which time the terrorists get ample time to net work their organization and increase their terrorist activities.

However looking to the present status of global/ local terrorism activities, some of the major remedial measures are to be taken as follows-

1) Come up with stringent policy and action to suppress them with iron hand irrespective of any political affiliation if they have established if any.

2) Cowardice approach of the ruling class should be totally discarded, as they should not stop the prosperity of greater number people for the malignant effect of negligible number of terrorists

3) Country's long-term development should not be compromised for the vested interest of few terrorists, for which the ruling class should apply 'mind bending' process with iron hand for the interest of the country.

4) Army. Police etc should be fully trained and with the determination of the government's will power, local terrorism activities can be easily controlled. No time should be wasted in negotiating with them.

5) The local people should be trained to facilitate police to remove terrorism.

6) No war of words or talks with such criminals should be taken up, which will indicate the

weakness of ruling community. Advantage will be taken by such demons.

7) It is a fact that the local terrorists cannot stand up before the mighty power of the government.

8) It is time that the government initiates stringent "mind bending" exercise to curb terrorism, which is possible if there is strong will power. It the question of exterminating lives of thousands of people for few mad people-the terrorists by adopting soft approach to them. If we do this History will not excuse us. For long term eradication of terrorism "mind mending' exercise need to be taken up. Between our birth and death how much resource we need to satisfy us? Before we calculate this, we must learn and know that when we die, we do not take any resource from our earth. To satisfy our needs we need security personal, food, shelter, livelihood, socio-economic, comfort-to satisfy us but not at the cost of others that means comfort with a sense of enoughness so that other members of our community are not deprived of resources to fulfill their basic needs and happiness-a mental state of equilibrium. All these are possible only if we can converge security, comfort and happiness with anti- matter elements-Truth, Order and Harmony.

17
Peace

FAMILY & PEACE

The foundation of Peace is the FAMILY. Without peace in family, peace cannot be established at any level. To restore family structure, the first step to improve relationship between husband and wife. The relationship is detoriating day by day mainly because of stresses created from over-materialistic culture. Both physical as well as spiritual relationship between husband and wife are on the decline. Sexual component of physical relationship plays a major role. Extra-marital relationship accompanied by clash of ego, lack of understanding and adjustment between husband and wife etc have led to collapse of family, which is the foundation of social structure. Wife and husband should be made equal partners without any gender discrimination. If the wife becomes an alpha woman, the husband should gladly accept without being jealous and readjust his mind-set with a positive attitude to avoid any conflict. The wife should also take appropriate care of the husband's psychic and share everything in a positive manner with her husband. The intensity of love, affection, caring and sharing should increase between the couple so that two wheels of family-the wife and husband run on the rails of life harmoniously.

With restoration of old-time husband-wife relationship with positive changes needed to adjust the forces of over-materialistic culture which will stabilize the family creating peace in every member of the family, which will contribute to community and global peace. Let us work together to achieve this objective so that peaceful communities are established in the world. Let us adopt Family as a powerful Social Institution.

Because of breakdown of family, the community is at risk. Sense of community is declining. Individualism is on the rise. With this environment how to create propeace community? Individualism is an accompaniment of utilitarianism. The "inert" matter is occupying more and more space as a result space for "live" matter is declining. Human mind which creates everything has become more reptiles even to the extent of killing itself. A radical change is urgently needed to change the human mind for bringing equilibrium in secretion of hormones in human body and neurotransmitters in human mind. We have to be scientifically aware of this to expedite the pace of desired change towards peace. With peace of family, world peace will prevail. This basic is to be accepted, if the humanity desire to live in a peaceful environment.

18

Peace

SPIRIT OF PEACE

1.6 millions years have passed since Homo sapiens appeared in the planet earth. They have developed many ideas and innovations to sustain their existence in the earth through art, science, technology, economies, tradition, culture and values etc. Out of the "Ideas" developed many have yielded outputs both towards prosperity as well as destruction.

But unfortunately, the word "Peace" is misconceived till date by the humanity, for which "peacelessness state" is dominating more and more day by day through violence like extreme materialism, wars, crimes, conflicts and terrorism etc. The crux of the problem is that till date the peace is conceived as only absence of physical violence - which is the greatest blunder committed by the humanity in the evolution of human civilization. It is only highlighted, discussed and talked about after violence war or terrorism etc. After passage of time, when some negotiation is reached to curb /curtail physical violence activities, "Peace" is pushed back to a corner and it plays no role in the day to day activity of the humans till the next violence takes place. It is therefore high time that the concept of "spirit of peace" is rightfully conceived, and understood put for putting into practice all kinds of day to day human activities expressed through art, science, technology, economies, environment, society, tradition, culture and values etc.

The "Spirit of Peace" should be perceived and understood holistically with two components with which the universe is created. Peace energy is energy of positiveness and forms the nucleus of Absolute Energy of Consciousness which is "antimatter" in nature and interacts with "matter" to create the universe which in turn has created the human species besides other biotic and abiotic elements. This implies that two components – "matter" and "antimatter" interact to construct the universe including the planets and the life forms in the planet earth.

For understanding of common world citizens, both matter and antimatter collectively contribute to peace and violent processes. It is up to the human intelligence how the interaction can be transformed to a peace process. As already said it can be achieved if the human intelligence is recognized and accepted as a holistic one with integration of IQ, EQ and SQ. With such holistic concept of intelligence both matter and antimatter can be explored for "Creative construction" of individuals and the humanity as a whole. This has to be dealt within the framework of humanitarianism and environmentalism. It also calls for establishing "collective minds" so that Peace becomes the prime mover of all ideas and innovations developed by humans, where there will be no space available for any kind of violence. This is the true understanding of "Spirit of Peace" which will lead to sustainable peace culture promoting ethical prosperity. This implies that Peace should become a day to day activity both in thought and action as a result violence in any form will be totally curbed and wiped out making the growth of evolution of the planet earth and the humanity peacefully sustainable.

This perception of "Spirit of Peace" leads to conclude that peace is the BASIC LIFE SUPPORT SYSTEM (BLSS). When this is accepted and adopted in practice, it will be capable of fulfilling the basic needs of humanity as a whole in all respects. With only peace, food, portable water, air, land, shelter, livelihood, health, education and all other needs of life to live as human beings in the planet earth will be available with quality, equity and sustainability. Without peace, all these needs will be corrupted and violent making life gradually unfit to live in the planet earth. This is the TRUTH to be realized in the 21st century and as such a SOS call is given to all humans wherever they are living to imbibe this concept of "Spirit of Peace" to switch over from the present "creative destruction" to "Creative construction".

Today, the dominant words for ushering changes are awareness, capacity building, training and education. It is a matter of concern that each of these words is compartmentalized and not being acted upon holistically with interlinked relationship. Further, different generalized and professional education are designed and implemented with "one track" approach succumbing to pressure of mobocracy It is therefore of urgent need to think differently the broad concept of education designing step by step knowledge up-gradation system holistically linking to wisdom so that the "Spirit of Peace" flowers through practice of all kinds of educational programmes. It is therefore necessary to reform and redesign the education system with "Peace" as the cutting edge. In order to materialize the concept, Peace Education should be recognized globally at different stages /levels of human growth linked to the education system as a whole. Peace education is not one time education but it has to start from the mother's womb and continue throughout the life period and end in tomb. The Peace educations need to be designed from womb to tomb which implies that our genes are to be mutated to in-build "peace" in our human genome. This may take few generations for mutation of present genes to become "Peace genes" – both body cells and neurons establishing new metabolism process between the two.

Thus time has come now to restructure the meaning, structure and concepts in the curriculum of "Education system" to learn and practice the "art of peaceful living". Original meaning of "school" which has come from Greek is a "place of peace /leisure", which needs to be restored as quickly as possible to arrest the present trend of unprecedented violence in the globalization era. Unfortunately with the present system of education, majority of mankind live in stark poverty, struggling for survival without effective access to justice, resources and other basic needs as a result only few affluent people of the world have built the society for themselves without understanding the consequences of such actions which are anarchy, disorder and confusion Children, the future generation absorb the "spirit of violence" rather than "spirit of peace" and become perpetuator of violence. The spirit of violence is dominating in all institutional structures of the human society. In the family /house children fight among themselves to view the specific shows in the television which is mostly a mind polluting and disturbing audio-visual object considering the present telecast pattern which is gradually becoming more and more vulgar and violent. The children also observe the discord between their parents and the negative behavior pattern to satisfy their hunger for unlimited desires. Further relationship management in the family is also hardly taken care of. In the schools, the children do not find peace/leisure (original meaning of school) and they are overburden with a system that encourages securing only high marks in the subjects taught for pursuing a money fetching career. Thus from the schools the children learn their first lessons of violence. To quote R.D.Laing "child born today in UK stands ten times greater chance of being admitted to a mental hospital than a university". This is not only true for UK but for the entire world also, considering the present education system. The joy of learning in the schools and other higher educational institutions is taken away from the children. Education today is narrowing down into teaching of certain subject matters necessary for passing examinations to join the mad race of the corrupt society to earn more and more money by hook or crook which make them run after mirage of false prosperity. The behavior of adolescents in the education system is insensitive to the problems of the society as a result they become selfish and narrow minded lacking in true intellectual depth. They have been more and more taught how to increase their IQ only and the system is totally silent about EQ and SQ. This make them susceptible to be violent and to corrupt social pressures which they are not been empowered to fight against such undue stress in the schools and universities. The excellence of few students cannot make up for millions of students who have imbibed the spirit of violence. School shoot outs, alcohol, sex, jealousy and intolerance etc between students are aggravating day by day as we stress cognitive learning in the schools / colleges at the cost of children's emotional, social, moral and humanistic values etc. The educational institutions have now been fully unethically commercialized and act as platforms of imbalance learning which is evident today in the form of youth unrest with their anti-social attitudes and behavioral problems. Under such decaying process of education system throughout the world it is time to think about a new system of education. The new perception of "education" should be based on foundation of peace. The present perception of education for pursuing only a career/profession needs to be modified to incorporate EQ and SQ in addition to IQ. It should be based on (a) values, non-violence ethics for resolving conflicts and promoting solidarity (b) social-justice ethics for distributing wealth, resources and power equitably and for promoting human relationship than ensure equal opportunity and respect (c) ecological sustainability – ethics for measuring the appropriateness of the impact of human activities on earth's life support systems and for ensuring earth's rights (d) participatory decision making ethics for democratic decision making and civic responsibility. (e) Application and evaluation of the above frameworks on a continuous basis. Basing on this cutting edge of "education", all educations like art, science, technology, management, and all other professional/non-professional courses now being run should be restructured and redesigned accordingly. The above five components form the cutting edge of the proposed new education system which will undoubtedly ensure "peace" as a critical constituent of education. Only this approach can bring sustainability accompanied by peace in the education system. Basing on such new "educational framework perception" all the curriculum of different subjects and professions in education from nursery level to highest level of education need to be reformed globally; which will in course of time develop social, economic and ecological peace without any violent ingredient. THIS IS WHAT THE PEACE EDUCATION IS ALL ABOUT. This will empower the world citizens not only to acquire true knowledge and pursue a career/lifestyle in consonance with the principles of BLSS (Basic life support life system) – the Peace. With strong determination and courage of humanity only, it is possible to work out ways of incorporating this new perception of education in the programmes and curriculums of all kinds of courses at all levels to pursue career/lifestyle from school onwards to acquire knowledge to improve quality of personal, social and professional life that will contribute to transformation of human society from the present peacelessness to sustainable peace. Once this is achieved the human genes will mutate in course of time to change the brain parts and central nervous system in the evolutionary process of human species, which is so special for the planet earth. The neural plate of the baby in the mother's womb will be imprinted with positive and peace impulses so that a peaceful human being will come out to the world to think and act "peace" through which he/she can bring prosperity uniformly distributed throughout the world. The concept of violence will be totally eradicated from the neural plate as a result the life that comes out from the mother's womb becomes a peaceful entity. A new and reformed human species vibrating with peace energy will emerge with this new perception of "education" to give a boost to sustainable and peaceful evolution of the earth/human species and other biotic and abiotic elements of the Biosphere.

19
Peace

SUSTAINABILITY OF PEACE

The truth is that, the humans cannot sustain themselves by eating money generated more and more through the present development models and distributed unevenly. This has given rise to violence in form of crimes, wars and terrorism etc which ultimately will end up in disappearance of homo sapiens from the biosphere. Thus Peace is to adopted as a critical input in the development process without which both Peace and Sustainable development will rise and fall together.

The moral message for the humanity is to adopt key principle that sustainable development which cannot be manifested and continued without Peace and as such each societal section of the globe should strive to achieve global sustainability within the real life framework of diversity in human society, in terms of varying environments, social practices and economies. The sustainability achieved by diversity of approaches should be unified to create truthfully a sustainable human society in the universe.

Lest we forget 9/11, we find the world is still terror-laden. In such a world can flowering of human mind concentrate on sustainable development? Human mind must evolve to replace terror-Laden world with peace-filled world to provide opportunity for sustainable development to spread its roots.

The United Nations General Assembly called for a Global meeting which was held on 22 December 1989 to devise strategies to halt and reverse the effects of environmental degradation "in the context of increased national and international efforts to promote sustainable and environmentally sound development in all countries". Consequent upon this decision, Agenda-21 was adopted by the United Nations Conference on Environment and Development on 14 June 1992. The recommendations of Agenda-21 should be studied in conjunction with Rio declaration on Environment and Development announced between 3-14 June 1992. These were also adopted at the conference known as the Earth Summit held on 3-14 June 1992 in Rio de Janeiro, Brazil.

The Agenda-21 holistically attempts to channelize human activities so that Development and Environment equilibrate with each other. With this approach all the countries of the world are urged upon to initiate actions at the grassroots level within a time frame.

The plan on implementation of the holistic package of sustainable development is still at flux, as a result expected and desired benefits are yet to be accrued to development and environment. In many countries, the idea of sustainable development has still to take root. Basing on Agenda-21, many deliberations have taken place throughout the world including the Millennium Development Goals(MDG) during last 15 years. In many countries 2015 goals are not fulfilled. In spite of all these steps, development taking place around the world is fragmented and not in conformity with the laws of ecology and environmental principles and in violation of recommendations of Agenda-21. It appears as if human minds are not adequately activated and tuned to design and work out an efficient programme for implementation of holistic sustainable development package. Although process of globalization aims at creating one global village, human actions are more and more dominated by "Self" or "Country" specific vested interest rather than developing a sense of empathy for all the people living in all the countries of the world. Acquisition of high level military strength like nuclear power, germ warfare etc are still given highest priority by some of the materially prospered countries which do not want to share their new knowledge and technologies with other countries. Even the Environmentally Sustainable Technologies (ESTs) developed are not shared amongst the countries. Some countries are yet to develop mindset to accept change from conventional technologies to ESTs (Environmentally sustainable Technology). Crimes, violence, war and terrorism are on the increase which indicates that the humans are giving more stress on "Creative destruction" than "Creative construction". Almost all prosperous and developing countries of the world have now victims of terrorism. Some of the main causes of terrorism are unsustainable development and psychic of few countries dominate over other countries. The terminology "Super Power" concept should be deleted from the political dictionary if the humanity believes in the principles of sustainable development. Such a mind set and change will expedite the implementation process of sustainable development. Thus without Peace, which includes security, stability, human rights, freedom, respect for natural and cultural diversity and values etc, sustainable development will remain as a slogan and a subject of deliberation only with war of words. This is quite evident from the action taken on implementation of the programme during last 15 years. The humanity must learn the lessons from the evolution of human civilization. Some of the political, military and cultural trends responsible for climate dominated by absence of Peace, given rise to wars and preparation for wars are like unilateralism, downplaying of collective political responsibility, growing and increasingly desperate economic disparity between world's rich and poor, military dominance and competition to acquire nuclear and germ war fare etc for mass destruction and last but not the least is the cultural dominance of greed and selfishness etc will make the development unsustainable and violent. Thus Peace and sustainable development will rise and fall together.

Learning the lessons from evolution of human civilization it is time now to recognize the role of Peace and its applications for sustainable development. Peace Technology is one of the most important tools recently invented to ensure preparation of an efficient and effective implementation programme to achieve sustainability for all kinds of development globally and locally. The Law of Peace Technology is defined as the technology of generation of psychic energy in three integrative forms of material and non-material consciousness force of: (1) techniques and intelligence of natural philosophical process of convergence of responses of "collective minds". (2) Eternity of truth, order and harmony (3) biospherism and humanitarianism determining level of and preferential order as security, comfort with a sense of enoughness and happiness. The security is all inclusive comprising personal, food, shelter, health, education, livelihood and environment. The comfort must be accepted with a "sense of enoughness" so that unlimited greed by few are replaced by satisfaction of basic need for all the people living in the world. Happiness is number of desires fulfilled divided by number of desires entertained. Unlimited desires bring more sorrow than happiness, which is the output of both "Matter" and "spirit". Desire should be limited to the concept of "Sense of enoughness" so that larger section of the people in the world does not suffer because of accumulation of benefits of development from the resources by a small of group of people in the world. The non-matter components of Peace are Truth, Order and Harmony which when blended with security, comfort and happiness in appropriate proportion will give rise to sustainable peace and development. Thus Peace Technology is nothing but a powerful tool of blending of "Science of Matter" with "Science of Spirituality". Science of matter and its application to produce various goods have been fully understood and adopted by the humanity. But it is time now to accept peace as an objective input to all kinds of development to be produced from the science of matter. The key concept of Peace Technology is convergence of Science of matter with Science of Spirituality to achieve sustainable development in true sense. Peace is an integral element of science of spirituality – a science to be recognized and applied by the humans for sustainable development.

From the scientific point of view spirituality is a higher form of energy within which other forms of energy like "inert" and "conscious" energy flow into the matter to create various kinds of goods and life forms. The present general perception that spirituality is something abstract or religious should be removed from the mind for dynamic interaction of "matter and spirit" which only can result in sustainable development. This concept forms the foundation of Peace Technology. The Ten commandments of Peace Technology are to be built into the development system to make it sustainable which are as follows:-

I.   Respect and worship the Mother Nature (the ecology), the supreme god-who is sustaining both biotic and a biotic world. "Matter" and "Non-matter" development are to be given equal emphasis. In other words, blending "Science of Matter" with "Science of Spirituality" is essential for Peace and sustainable development.

II. Recognize that the basic principle of sustainability is energy of peace acquired through activation of "consciousness" (subduing reptile mind and activating mammalian and cortex mind) of matter-life-mind for turning to a simpler ecological life with strengthening of "family bond" (well knitted children, parents and grandparents), "social justice" and "community living" systems, for evolving a methodology for acquiring "inner", "domestic" and "global peace". "Mind mending" exercise to be started from the mother's womb – leading to less and less "Mind bending "options.

III. Commit to the only process of "Sustainable development through Peace" and "Peace through sustainable development" and not after violent outburst like war, terrorism, poverty etc. and turning from a purely ("matter" de linked from "spirit") growth oriented thinking for initiating the process of peaceful and sustainable development.

IV. Dedicate ourselves to Biosphere peace characterized by unity in diversity, equity and sustainability that can only lead to peace of humanity and other life forms imbibing the spirit and imprinting in our minds the "oneness" of the world and human family- thus converging "development" with "spiritualism", resulting in real sustainable development.

V. Adopt principles of "one world" and recognize ourselves first as members of "Commonwealth of Nature" and then as members of "Commonwealth of Nations" so that present psychic of "creative destruction" is replaced by "creative construction.

VI. Use our intellect and emotions for all kinds of human activities and endeavors with the convergence of ecology, economy and ethics linked to socio-political and evolutionary dynamics, rejecting present irrational time calculus; adopting 28 days moon thirteen months civil calendar. The first day of magnetic moon on July 26 will be the first day of the new 13 months calendar. July 25 of the present calendar will be day out of time which will be celebrated as "Peace Day" throughout the word. This will bring about a positive and dynamic change in the "psychic" of human mind and behavior. In order to adopt the Peace Calendar and implementation of recommendations of Agenda-21, the status of political leaders to be uplifted to true leaders of universalization of sustainable and peaceful human society, through adoption of principles of Peace Technology.

VII. Change our behavior pattern in tune with harmonics and wisdom within the framework of social, moral and human values, rejecting extreme form of materialistic culture and moving towards the energy of "Spirit". This calls for Peace Education as a course in school and colleges from the childhood to the highest level of education. Peace to be incorporated as a "subject" in all the faculties which will be designed differently at various levels.

VIII. Recognize "Peace" as objective (not subjective) which can be acquired by adopting suitable "one world technology" of development models from individual, family, societal and global level, basing on the principles of creation of the universe and the evolution process of the ecology and humanity.

IX. Adopt three steps to promote individual to global peace as security, comfort (with sense of enoughness) and happiness for the biosphere and all its life forms with convergence of techniques and intelligence of responses of "collective minds" with the eternity of truth, order and harmony. Convergence of humanitarianism and biosphereism for redirecting the course of present irrational human actions towards sustainability.

X. Commit ourselves to the natural philosophical process of "Self-realization" and "bio-centric" attitude by igniting "inwardness" to contribute and materialize the concept of "one world" and "one human family" to free the humanity from the psychic of confrontation, innovation of unethical and antibiotic technologies, wars, terrorism, discrimination, inequity and poverty etc. to put a halt to "global slumming" and other kinds of violent outbursts to give chance to peace and sustainable development to rule the biosphere.

Sustainability of Peace

20
Peace

ENERGY & PEACE

Einstein energy equation $E=mc^2$ perceives that when a body has a mass, it has certain amount of energy even it is at rest and does not have any form of potential energy, chemical energy etc; it still has that amount of energy. The simplistic interpretation of this equation is that maximum amount of energy obtainable from an object is equivalent to the mass of object multiplied by square of speed of light. This equation was crucial in the development of atom bomb. Basically this equation is applicable to matter for production of both constructive and destructive goods.

Subsequently Einstein's thought process tried to introduce cosmological constant, solution of the field equation, vacuum field equation but it appears that he was not convinced and satisfied basing on which he came up with a providential statement – "A human being is a part of whole, called universe, a part limited to time and space, he experiences himself his thoughts and feelings has something separated from the rest – a kind of optical illusion of "consciousness". This delusion is a kind of prison for us, restricting us to our personal desires and to affection for few persons nearest us. Our task must be to free from ourselves from the prison of by widening our circle of compassion to embrace all leaving creatures and the whole of Nature of beauty".

This is the essence of sustainable development and within this framework of Einstein's thought process we have to answer the question that "what is a universe?" To answer this question we have to apply the concept of "Natural Philosophy" to clarify our perception of universe through a systematic study. Universe is nothing but an infinity source of consciousness energy/ cosmic energy/spiritual energy having ability to create forces to interact with the matter of the universe on a continuous basis.

The forces create "Everything" from the infinity energy of spirituality whose fundamental particle is "spiriton", having the nucleus of Peace Consciousness energy around which the particles of universal mind namely "Thought" and "Emotion" revolve. If thought and emotion become highly negative and go out of control of the nucleus, both body and mind of a person become radical, as a result the person is filled with negative energy. Such persons become violent and reactive with full of negativities. This shall be perceived clearly and scientifically to create awareness amongst the world citizens to minimize number of such person to save the world and the humanity from violent forces.

Spiritual energy / universal peace consciousness energy is the vortex of energy pyramid and radiates to different levels for creation of different kinds of matter/spirit objects. The base of the pyramid is dominated by matter and inert energy, which is a lower level of energy through which the humanity produces all kinds of material goods ignoring their spiritual components. Time is ripe to give spatial and scientific dimension to spirituality and incorporate it in the sustainable development programs.

The statement of Einstein has elevated him from the status of reputed scientist to the status of Natural Philosopher. He perhaps realized that his pure scientific equation of energy is not complete and will not heal the humanity for which he conceived that a human is a part of universe and used words like thoughts feelings, consciousness, compassion, and Nature of Beauty etc. If he would have lived longer, he might have come out with and energy equation blending both matter, consciousness and above all the spirituality. Basically, the energy which has the ability to create a force over a distance sometime in the future. The universe is a holistic unit of energy and matter. All kinds of energy including inert energy flow from the spiritual energy into the matter to produce goods to meet the material needs of humanity. Positive spiritual energy and universal peace consciousness energy are synonymous in nature. From this energy conscious energy or the spirit energy is transmitted to create life forms including humans with both positive and negative attitudes. Both the conscious energy and inert energy are interlinked to create a force over distance sometime in future. The force is primarily conceived as interplay and exchange of energy spirit and matter. The Absolute consciousness energy is also synonymous with Universal peace consciousness energy.

From this prime source of energy, there is continuous transmission, recycling of various kinds of lower level energy in different masses which result in creation, dissolution and recreation of universe, human civilization and all other objects. Considering the Einstein's providential statement using the words consciousness, compassion etc, my equation of Absolute Energy of Consciousness has been invented. The equation conceives the smallest of the smallest particle to the power of energy and matter when multiplied by time infinity results in Absolute Energy of Consciousness. The equation considers the concept of "Ultimate reality" of life and universe and its deeper and systematic study which has resulted in an Absolute Energy of consciousness field from which the peace energy flows to both conscious and inert matters. My equation if adopted as the prime source of Absolute energy which within the frame work of Einstein's energy equation holds good, will justify the thought process of Einstein on consciousness and compassion.

This also perhaps fulfills the dream of Einstein to remove optical delusion of consciousness to free the human from the prison to widen their circle of compassion and embrace al living creatures with peace energy / spiritual energy. This will simultaneously facilitate the humans to create products of matter linked to spirit to ensure sustainability of all development efforts taken up by the humanity, simultaneously creating a culture of peace.

In my energy equation, time has been conceived as a infinity moving energy characterized by healing, purifying and unifying which are the essential factors for ensuring sustainable development and peace. It is therefore humbly submitted that while designing processes of all human activities, peace and sustainability of goods produced from the processes can only be achieved with collective application of Einstein's and my energy equation.

This can also be accepted as a unified theory of spiritual, conscious, peace and inert energy which interact with matter within the framework of time infinity for ensuring peaceful and sustainable development. The world citizens are urged upon to understand and apply the blending of both the equations so that "ultimate reality" of life and universe can be achieved. Peaceful Sustainable development and Peace are the two most important components of the ultimate reality.

Energy and Peace

21
Peace

INNER PEACE

Both the universe and humanity are now sick, mainly because of declining level of cosmic energy in production of various goods, as a result Peace and sustainable development are eluding the universe and the mankind. Time has come now to heal both of them for their sustainability. Humans, because of their more and more destructive actions are responsible for such sickness. We have to initiate curative measures. All kinds of medicines inducted to diseased are attempts to create additional positive energy so that positive energy neutralize in negative energy of diseased; as a result healing takes place.

Let us probe first the health and sickness of the universe. As the universe is a holistic unit of varieties of energy beginning from Absolute consciousness energy to inert energy (matter) through which our solar system and stars and all kind of things in the universe are created. All these creative things / spirits of the universe establish inter and intra relationship for their systems to run. If the systems during such process of interaction and relationship building generate more negative energies, the function of the universe is adversely affected.

There are millions of energy centers in the universe as well as channels through which to and fro transmission of energy takes place. In addition to such external intervention, natural evolution process of the universe also generates positive and negative energy. Without external intervention, the negative energy generated in the natural evolution process is generally neutralized through an auto-clock system. The neutralization of negative energy provides creation of more positive energy for increasing the longevity of the universe. Today the external intervention generates high level of negative energy mainly because of unsustainable development and human actions not in conformity with the laws of Nature. This has increased the sickness of universe and its millions of energy centers and channels due to in equilibrium of energy balance. Thus if the human actions / spirits are restructured to generate less negative energy, the universe will be relatively healthy.

This takes us to probe human energy structure. There are seven energy centers in the human body which generate energy in the body. The body is attached to a meridian – pipe (nadi –channel) that enables the energy to flow into and out of it. There are almost 7200 such channels in the human body. The centers absorb the energy, channel it to form the aura (power) of the person and then the energy starts to flow towards different organs via the nadi- channel. The power energised at the centres determines the size of the aura and the quantity of energy. The thoughts and emotions of a person enable the energy centers to accept the energy of likewise vibrations for which the quality of one's aura depends on these vibrations. Negative thoughts or emotions adjust the energy centers to accept negative information, which has adverse affect on the body to accept unclean energy. It makes a human more violent prone devoid of humanitarian qualities, as a result the peace energy flows out of body.

There are seven energy centers in the body as a single and holistic entity with diversified units. Spirit, body, consciousness, peace, violence, earth, stars and the whole universe etc are in continuous interaction and are subject to the law of cause and effect. From here it can be concluded that everything that happens to a person is the direct result of law of cause and effect – in Hindu philosophy it is known as "Karma". The status of energy centers not only affect a person's bodily organs but also certain aspects of his "karma" in this life time and/or may be subsequent life.

22
Peace

PEACE AND HUMAN RIGHTS

In the 21st century, it is an important task to redefine Peace. Its meaning "absence of war" needs to be supplemented. When we look around the world today, we find total chaos, meltdowns accompanied by high level of violence/terror etc. Some of the facts justifying this statement are like- UNICEF reported in 2006, the number of children under fourteen years of age who are suffering from AIDS is 2.1 million. In some fifty poor countries such as Chad, Guinea, Bissau, Sierra Leone, Liberia, Afghanistan, and Somalia, one of every six children dies before reaching the age of five, due to lack of health services like vaccination, clean drinking water and malnutrition. These children die of extreme poverty. Inter National Labor Organization (ILO) published in 2005 that 126 million children in the world are engaged in performing dangerous work. Hunger, shelterlessness, lack of access to education, health facilities besides other basic social-economic needs etc are not only dominating but increasing at a faster rate giving rise to various kinds of violence. Other issues like global warming, resource depletion and loss of biosphere peace are speeding up further deteriorating quality of human race. Terrorism and other kinds of serious crimes like school shootouts, genocide, drug addiction, violence against women etc are also on the rise.

How the present definition of Peace can be justified when 75% wealth of the world is in the hands of 1% of the population in the world. In developing countries, power brokers give false promises to people and use muscle and money power to grab power at the cost of all ethics and values. In a country like India, millions of people are born homeless. They get married on streets, live on streets and die on streets; whereas the most expensive and luxurious hotels and homes exist for only five percent of the population. Redefining Peace is the challenge of 21st century to face the reality that humanity shares a common fate on a crowded planet. It needs basically a holistic base on which all human activities need to be redesigned. Thus Peace in 21st century is to be defined as convergence of "Science of Matter"(Security from personal, food, shelter, livelihood and all other basic socio-economic needs; comfort with a sense of enoughness and happiness) with "Science of Spirituality"(Truth, Order and Harmony). Spirituality as a Science has not been conceived by humanity yet; as a result we are confronted with all kinds of meltdowns, terror and a process of stratification of human family leading to a cruel and violent world. Peace will not elude mankind, the moment "Science of Spirituality" is adopted as objective and integrated with Science of Matter to produce all kinds of products and services needed for prosperity and comfortable living with a sense of enoughness. I am fully aware that adoption of this CHANGE is extremely difficult unless some leader/s with total self-less dedication and commitment to humanitarian causes come forward to remold the human mindset and convince the humans that this is the only definition of Peace that will provide them at all levels through creative constructive activities. In my humble way, I have taken up this challenge and I hope in course of next few generations this concept of Peace will be built into all human endeavors/activities so that a violent/terror free world vibrating with Peace Culture will emerge. With this new definition of Peace, the framework of ethical peace is to be constructed with humanitarian values and corresponding Human Rights. Peace and Human Rights are two sides of one coin. Universal declarations of Human Rights have announced that

"Everyone has the right to life, liberty, and security of persons.....No one shall be subjected to torture or to cruel, inhuman or degrading treatment and punishment....... Everyone has the right to a standard of living adequate for the health and wellbeing of himself and his family, including food, clothing, housing, medical care and necessary social services......Everyone is entitled to a social and international order in which......rights and freedoms can be fully realized." On December 10, 1948, UN adopted and proclaimed Universal Declaration of Human Rights with 30 Articles. More than 68 years have passed since the Declaration, but unfortunately till date government's/Nation's obligation to ensure implementation of the issues of Human Rights remain a distant dream It is now time in the beginning of 21st century to integrate Peace and Human Rights and apply to all human activities relating to development, poverty, livelihood and land, environment, education, food, health, housing, the aged, children, differently abled, discrimination, ethnicity, indigenous people, minorities, migrant workers, race, refugees, reproductive health, religion, sexual orientation, women, work and workers and disarmaments etc. Human Right issues are to be deliberated and implemented with all seriousness by governments which gain their legitimacy through votes of people and respect for human rights and not through votes of people and voting boxes. Humanitarianism is the foundation of human rights and is to be applied to any civilization and culture. Violation of Human Rights such as cultural relativism, religion and ideology etc should be viewed as criminal action and should be strictly dealt with-even to the dismissal of such governments enjoying majority. Democracy is "rule by people". They have the power to choose their leaders for living in a society characterized by justice and freedom. But unfortunately this is not happening. In most of Asian countries true democracy eludes the region, mainly due to non-integration of Peace and Human Rights components in the development process.

Today development is unsustainable and violent as issues relating Peace and Human Rights do not form integral part of development. Development can only be sustainable and "inclusive" when peace is blended with human rights components. In addition to the recommendations at global level, I suggest some of simple ideas to achieve Human Rights at the grassroots level considering the unification of Life, Habitat and Peace-

(a) Safety & Security of life from any kind of violence (b) Access to high standard of Health service (c) Access to "Adequate Shelter" (d) build a physical environment that provides pure air to inhale, pure water to drink and unpolluted land to stay. (e)Provide opportunity to live in "Green" and not in concrete jungle. (f) Provide all facilities and regulatory measures in the Habitat so that air, water, land, and noise pollution are totally eliminated. (h) Build Habitats, where people are not killed by accidents.(h) design Habitats in pedestrian and cycle scale linked to Mass Transit system(MTS) (i) change the land use planning of Habitats to provide life-friendly physical, economic, social, family and environmentally stimulating space (j) blend spirit with matter to access Peace (k) Make Peace an integral component of Development (l) create a suitable surrounding where every citizen of the Habitats of the world gets nutritious food to eat and live. Hunger must be wiped out. (m) Provide adequate opportunity for the people to work so that no one remains idle (n) do not provide free food/goods to people to make them idle, which tempt them to live a life of vices.(o) give education highest priority and make it from "womb to tomb" igniting the consciousness of mind instead of a mechanical education system.

These are some of the ideas of Human Rights for implementation at Habitat and grassroots level to satisfy the hunger of happiness and peace.

While deliberating ideas of Human Rights at grassroots level, we have to find solutions to the 21st Century's serious problems of meltdowns and terrorism which can only be solved with the application of new definition and principles of Peace and Human Rights(both at global and grassroots level) and with unification of Life, Habitat and Peace.

We live in the complex world

With words & promises

With pain & pleasure Devoid of basic rights

Of air, water and land

Life is exploited

Unable to design a live Habitat

Of happiness & peace.

23
Peace

PEACE POEMS

DEFINING PEACE

The first smile of newly born baby is peace
Mother's love for the baby is peace
Parenting the baby is peace
Become a part of growing process of the baby is peace
Peace is opposite of violence
Peace is Truth, Order and Harmony
Peace is love, affection and empathy
Equity, sustainability and eco-friendly
Peace is a source of energy
Creating spiriton and then
Proton, neutron and electron
Peace creates life
Consciousness is a product of peace and
That of the universe and the life
Peace is infinite and time and space less
But creates temporal objects
Peace is a bridge between 'science and spirituality"

Peace provides life-support systems
Creating resources and ecological equilibrium
Peace creates prosperity
With adoption of appropriate technology
Peace is divine and material
Peace stimulates wisdom
And peaceful behavior
To develop ecology and human systems
Sustaining universal laws
OH humans accept and develop
The definition of peace for
Creating one world-one peaceful global human family
Without violence, wars and terrorism

THE PEACE, ECOLOGY AND HOMO SAPIENS:

Universal laws Give
Birth to Mother Nature
A Unique blending of beauty
Serenity, resources and harmony
Peace is inbuilt to Mother Nature
The sun rise, sun set and bounty of
Flora and fauna express peace
Stimulating the innerness of
Life forms transforming them
Reptile to mammalian ones
Ecology, the science of relationship
Between life forms and their environment
Based on the energy of peace
Creates and dissolves
To be again part of universal peace
A wonderful and beautiful universe
Would have been there
With colorful peace and ecology
But the misadventure of
Homo sapiens
Greedy and crooked
Destroy peace and ecology
Without peeping into their consciousness
Believing more and more on virtuality
As days pass by civilization after civilization
Inviting the "doomsday"
Which is not far away today

SEPTEMBER 11, 2001 AND PEACE:

September 11, 2001
A day in human civilization
A dark day of
Terror
Dissolving thousands of lives
Babies, children, old and youths
Without any reasons or rhymes
Buried the innocent souls in the WTO
The world's most powerful Trade center
Of mightiest Americans
Who with all their wealth and prosperity
Succumbed to un precedent violence of death
Prosperity devoid of peace failed to
Counter the violence
Giving a call for
A new America's war
Will it be a war of violence or
A war of Peace
The science of time still not understood fully
Will document in history the form in which
The event will be acknowledged by the posterity
But the message that PEACE is always victorious
Will continue to rule the humanity till life continues
In the biosphere.

MILLENNIUM DEVELOPMENT GOALS:

Without fear, desperation and terrorism
And with love, affection, compassion, and equilibrium
To live with security, comfort and happiness
And with truth, order and harmony
But development goals adopted in last two millenniums
Have failed creating more and more pessimisms
Raising serious apprehension
For survival of humans
In the planet earth and cosmic world
Instead of creative construction
Creative destruction has increased manifold
In the last two millenniums
Because of in equilibrium relationship between
"spiriton and atom"
"non-matter and matter"
and gradually loss of reins
by the mind (The driver)
on the five senses
human body
leading it to the path of suicide
and to a process self combustion of matter
Reverting back to a stage of status-quo
Of "nothingness" which was there before
"The Big Bang"
With absolute peace of spiriton of universe
Without giving any scope to Big Bang
Development goals of third millennium calls for
Evaluation of goals of last two millenniums
So that appropriate intellectualism

Without any discrimination and inequity in use of atom
And learning the principles of spiriton linked to atom
Deepening our roots with oneness,
friendship, compassion, cooperation
Love, caring, sharing, tolerance and value education
Truth, order and harmony to be inbuilt to goals
To meet the material needs of all
With the principle of humanitarianism
and biosphereism
All such elements constitute peace technology concept
Collectively represent spiriton and atom oncology
To erase violence from the mind and
Root out terrorism from the mortal world
OH humans accept millennium development goals
As peace with its sources and
constituents of technology
To ensure saga of humanity
To continue in the biosphere
Through designing human activities
both for biosphere and human peace
for making millennium development goals
peaceful, sustainable and vibrant
free of crime, violence and terrorism root.

A CALL TO THE MOTHER-TO-BE OF THE WORLD:

Adam and Eve
Adam is seed
Eve is soil
Seeds put in Eve
makes Eve pregnant
Mother-to-be
The seed and soil
relationship results
in creation of a life
Man and Women relation
like seed and soil passages
through different stages
of childhood, adulthood and old
Nothing remains static
science of time is least understood
And in no time childhood transforms to old age
Human body craves for satisfaction
of biological, sexual, and metabolical needs
Manage the three stages of life
Especially the adulthood
Enjoy material objects, sex, places
And relationship
In a responsible manner
to ensure bright future of your progeny
After all that mother-to- be stage arrives
to create a new life
only with the energy of PEACE
Understand and cultivate your mind
remembering that an offspring is not
the product of vulgar sex

Neither it is product of disco or dating
Quality of offspring is determined by
internal impulses of mother's body
and family, community and society impulses
to mould his/her life-body-mind relationship
here the peace energy modulates
More the peace- consciousness energy
the child in the mother's womb vibrates
with peace energy
resulting in creation of a peaceful
human being without any violence mind
oh mothers -to- be of the world
learn the techniques of infusing peace
energy to your child in the womb
to create a peaceful offspring
who will enrich your life with real
joy and making you proud
who will spread the fragrance of peace
throughout the world
to make our planet earth "Green and Peace"-A
place to live in peace and prosperity
Will you not do it?
Do it to spend a meaningful life

FOR CHILDREN - CALL TO CHILDREN OF THE WORLD:

OH CHILDREN
YOU ARE SO SWEET
SO PURE AND SERENE
YOUR HEART, MIND AND SOUL
SPREAD FRAGRANCE OF
PEACE HAPPINESS AND EMPATHY
RETAIN THE FRAGRANCE
WHEN YOU GROW UP
FOR IGNITING YOUR INNER PEACE
THE SOURCE OF "CONSCIOUS ENERGY"
THAT MAKE YOUR LIFE-BODY-MIND
TO INTERACT WITH "MATTER"
FOR ENJOYING WORLDLY COMFORTS
OF SECURITY AND HAPPINESS
BUT COMFORT FROM "MATTER"
GIVES YOU VIRTUAL HAPPINESS
WHEREAS REAL HAPPINESS COMES FROM
"NON-MATTER"-LOVE, AFFECTION, EMPATHY
TOLERANCE, CONCERN FOR OTHERS
SENSE OF ENOUGH NESS OF
MATERIALISTIC PRODUCTS
SO THAT YOU SHARE AND CARE FOR
OTHER CHILDREN OF THE WORLD
TO ACQUIRE ULTIMATE OBJECT OF
YOUR LIFE- THE PEACE
TO LEARN MORE, CULTIVATE YOUR MIND
ASK YOUR TEACHERS
TO EXPLAIN YOU THE INGREDIENTS
OF PEACE
SO THAT TEACHERS BECOME AWARE
AND DEVELOP YOU AS

A PEACEFUL HUMAN BEING
SPREADING THE SWEETNESS OF PEACE
WITHIN YOU AND ALL AROUND YOU
CREATING ONE WORLD-ONE
PEACEFUL GLOBAL FAMILY.
THEN ONLY YOU SURVIVE PEACEFULLY
IN THIS BEAUTIFUL WORLD.

ABOUT THE AUTHOR

Born in a remote village Dumuka, Kendrapara district, Odisha, India in 1936, he has faced immense turmoil in life from the childhood. He has seen poverty and was seriously affected by lack of amenities and facilities influencing his mental and physical health. But God came to his rescue. For having most sincerely served as an acclaimed, acknowledged, accomplished, admired and appreciated Administrator of Indian Institute of Travel and Tourism Management, Bhubaneswar in Ministry of Tourism, Government of India, during 1997-1999, from which prestigious position, he has most gracefully retired, for having also done wonderfully well. He most commendably served as the Commissioner-cum-Secretary to Government of Odisha in Housing and Urban Development Department, in the functioning of which he brought tremendous improvement during the tenure of five years. During this period, he started Building Centre Movement, Ecological Engineering for cleaning waste water of cities and towns, participated with Government of India for 73rd and 74th Constitution Amendment Act of India, and cleared projects of DFID (then ODA) for slum less town. HE introduced Fly ash brick in the state. He blended Community/NGOS works with Government schemes. In Tribal Department, he cleared Development scheme from IFAD for Kasipur block. He worked with World Bank Team for ten towns of the state. He created many Institutions like SUDA, Odisha Water Supply & Sewerage Board etc. He discharged his duties effectively as Vice Chairman Bhubaneswar Development Authority and started housing schemes for the first time sponsored by government. He brought about perceptible changes in the city of Bhubaneswar. He also works as Managing Director of Odisha Milk Federation and Aska Sugar factory. He was Director, Information & public Relation to Government of Odisha for two terms. He also served as Registrar, Co-Operative Societies and brought about many reforms. During his tenure as District Collector & Magistrate in a tribal district, he started an innovative scheme of "Grassroots Management" during 1980-83 which is now enlarged to SHG (Self Help Groups) to all the states of the country. An I.A.S officer of rare repute, he served the poor people of the state in most dedicated manner- and almost become part of the poor. Qualification wise, he is highly educated with B.sc(Bachelor of Science), B.E (Bachelor of Civil Engineering from Bombay University), and Post graduate in Town & Country Planning from School of Planning and Architecture (SPA), New Delhi. He has also undergone many management training from IIM, Bangalore, ASI, Hyderabad, NIU (National Institute of Urban Development), Delhi, Management Institute, Gurgaon etc. He has specialized in Peace, Environment and Habitat and Urban Development. He has published two books 1) Peace Technology 2) Peace Time Calendar; published by author house, Bloomington, Indiana, USA. He has been awarded with Peace Clinic Peace Prize Award in 2005 by Peace Clinic Institute, Oceanside, California, USA. Further he has also been awarded with Certificate of Recognition by USA Honor Society, New York, 2009 for his achievement of HIGHEST ORDER. He has also been nominated in to Presidential Who's Who 2009/10, New York for his outstanding achievement in Peace & Technology. He has also to his credit four international publication-1)Socialization of Human Settlement System: A strategy for bridging the food gap in the third world –UN conference on Human Settlement, 1976 2)Genes, Species, Ecosystem, Development & Urban Environment-published in book Management of Development-Growth with Equity by Association of Management Development, Institutions in South Asia 1998 published by Excel Books, India 3)Reconnecting Man with Nature-Role of Tourism published by Nova Science Publications, New York, USA 4) Ecological Engineering for waste water Management published by International Ecological Society, Switzerland and University of Kalyani, India, 2000; published in the book Waste Recycling and Resource Management in the Developing Countries.

He is now working as Professor (Emeritus) Peace & Ekistics in Piloo Mody College of Architecture, Cuttack, Odisha, India. His web site is www.worldpeacetech.com which may be visited to know more about his work. All such achievements mentioned could not have been possible without HIS blessings.

Epilogue

Life generated million years back in the lap of Mother Nature. But, unfortunately the humans for the sake of "self-development" is in continuous war with Nature. In the war Nature is always the winner. Humans are under attack with weapons like climate change, global warming, terrorism etc. As the behavior of humans become unbearable, Mother Nature has now developed a weapon "Zika" which will redesign the humans. With the weapon, the head of the baby in the mother's womb will be below average head size caused by failure of brain growth at normal rate. Head circumference will be measuring less than 31.5-32 cm at birth. Still this day about 41 countries have been attacked. This will reduce the intelligence of human, causing many aberrations in his functioning of spirit, mind and body. Similarly human habitat is evolved from caves with plenty of pure air, water and land to high rise skyscrapers endangering the life of Mother Nature which struck back snatching away basic needs of humans- habitats where no pure air, water and land is available. Such high tech habitats built by humans may be the cause of their extinction from the Biosphere. Peace is not evolving as it is sustainable from its origin. But the humans are fighting against peace creating a living environment totally unfit for human habitat.

The book advocates unification of Life, Habitat and Peace by blending of "Science of Spirituality" with "Science of

Matter" for construction of sustainable, prosperous and peaceful Habitats so that Life, Habitat and Peace are in harmony with each other and with the laws of Mother Nature.